From 'Play to Art

From Play to Art

George Szekely

HEINEMANN
Portsmouth, New Hampshire

Heinemann Educational Books, Inc.
361 Hanover Street
Portsmouth, NH 03801-3959

Every effort has been made to contact the copyright holders and students for permission to reprint borrowed material. We regret any oversights that may have occurred and would be happy to rectify them in future printing of this work.

Library of Congress Cataloging-in-Publication Data
Szekely, George E.
  From play to art / by George Szekely.
    p. cm.
  Includes bibliographical references.
  ISBN 0-435-08571-9
  1. Play. 2. Art—Study and teaching (Elementary)—Kentucky.

LB1137.S94 1991
372.5044'09769–dc20
                          91-19113
                          CIP

Design by Jenny Jensen Greenleaf.
Printed in the United States of America.
91 92 93 94 95 9 8 7 6 5 4 3 2 1

Dedication

To Dr. Laura Szekely, my wife, who has for the past twenty years
used her many talents and freely given her time to
make all my artistic dreamings reality.

Contents

◆

Preface

How do people select an area of research? Studies frequently comprise little more than a bibliography and a review of other writings, and the introductions to most offer few clues to their genesis. But an artist's research requires more immediate and personal involvement. Several observations led to my decision to keep a video camera at my side for the past three years so that I could record children's creative playing.

First, I noticed how young children create constantly and make art with everything. Children engage in any activity—whether packing lunch, setting a dinner table, or preparing toy soldiers for battle—as a great creative act. Chairs, raisins, and umbrellas all become props. It seemed to me that the art spontaneously played out at home in adventures and inventions was more varied in its uses of materials, more personal, and freer in invention than any school art I had ever observed. I also noticed that these artistic beginnings were closely related to independent, creative, adult behaviors that quickly disappear as children enter school. Children who arrive in school with infinite abilities for setting up experimental kitchens and conducting make-believe journeys to just about anywhere soon claim they are not good in art. They quickly lose, or perhaps forget, the richness of their inventions and the fertility of their own imaginations; instead, they wait for materials and ideas from their teachers. On entering school, young artists go unrecognized, their art views superseded by adult notions of "real" art.

In my video studies, I wanted not only to present the sources of children's art in all their variety of playing but also to call attention to these creative plays as art and, certainly, as the beginnings of children's vision and creative life. In their creations, I soon saw an art different from either that which we generally call children's art or that which is generally taught to children. What I recorded was an art different in media, approach, and attitude from adult art and more fascinating than the most avant-garde art inventions (which frequently use children's art as models). While filming, I was inspired by playful young artists and their often unnoticed inventions. Using throwaway media—for example, chewing gum, toothpaste, or potato chips—in temporary constructs such as play houses or dressing-up events, kids produce art that looks like play, happens too quickly, and is destroyed too soon, leaving no opportunity for even temporary display. It is hard to save art made with napkins or the foil of a candy wrapper. Film, however, seemed an appropriate medium for preserving these fleeting art forms.

It requires effort for art teachers to begin seeing children as artists and even colleagues, not as beginners to be taught everything about art. My film study does not provide a basis either for statistics or for specific school curricula, but it is testimony to children's at-home creative abilities before and during early school years. Each filmed episode provides an important window on early art sources, art choices, interests, skills, media, and so on, which teachers seldom consider when preparing art lessons or introducing art worlds. The film also furnishes great evidence that early art is intertwined with play, suggesting that we need to take a more serious look at play development and creativity as well as to rekindle play in the art class. The film further points up the importance of art teachers looking at art education in terms of self-education and of seriously studying home art or other art made without their guidance. Creative acts outside school prepare children for school art; thus the art teacher's self-preparation should not be the only concern. School art should not isolate children's art from their world and interests by imposing adult art and standards that are not the art deeds, language, or concerns of children.

Most people entering art teaching are relatively young and often have had few experiences with kids beyond the opportunities provided for observing them in school art classes. Future teachers need to observe children's plays and inventions outside of school. As a graduate student watching these films noted, the prerequisite for teaching art should be to have children of one's own in order to have time to appreciate their creativity outside the classroom. Yet even parents tend not only to ignore children's art but also to consider it an annoyance. Art in a bathtub "studio," for example, simply prolongs bath time; kids playing in any room are simply "making a mess"; plays at the dinner table are deemed impolite.

From Play to Art seeks to pay significant attention to children's play-oriented creativity, which is not only generally ignored but also considered trivial. The play approaches to art teaching described in this book were developed from the video studies and from many hours observing children at play. With the assistance of graduate students, plays moved into the schools as we began a two-year funded research project in four Kentucky elementary schools. We trained teachers and demonstrated playing in each art class. The project's first year was enthusiastically reviewed by colleagues and continues to inspire children in eighteen elementary schools. A new art emerged from this project—children's art played out in a variety of innovative media and techniques. Best of all, the art classes in our schools became the place to be. As one child said, "It is the place where kids star and incredible ideas rule." Another child simply remarked, "I never knew that so much fun is possible in school."

The book's plan of a play is straightforward. Chapter 1 presents the overall framework and proposes major play ideas. Chapter 2 is an inquiry into play environments: what makes them work and how to set them up. Chapter 3 considers materials of play invention that successfully challenge and inspire players. Chapter 4 considers the role of movement in play and art. Chapter 5 discusses play roles that can be practiced by both teacher and student performers. Chapter 6 focuses on the basic plays that we all enjoyed as children and begins to build play categories for art adaptations. Chapter 7 categorizes the themes most frequently found in children's playing and describes examples of artistic adaptations. Chapter 8 links spaces, materials, movements, and performance in a series of full-scale examples from our art classes. And the epilogue concludes the book by offering teaching tips and suggestions for play designs in school art programs.

Makeup and Disguise Portrait

ONE

Introduction

The first time I applied for a job in a university, I was asked to teach a demonstration lesson. Since I had been caught by surprise, the lesson evolved spontaneously.

I began by asking the students to get down on the floor with me and sit under their tables so that we could play house as we did as children. I began to recount my own memories of playing under tables as a child, describing the varieties of forts and vehicles I had assembled. Soon, these adult university students began enthusiastically sharing their memories of special and private spaces they had as children: clubhouses, secret corners in a garage, forts in their beds and under desks. They recalled dining-room chairs that had magically become trains, elegant thrones, or motorcycles.

Memories of early hiding places led to recollections of creating displays of things in special areas, arranging treasured toys and found objects on a shelf or in a certain corner of the bedroom. It became clear to all of us that our early play experiences had a connection with our approaches to art as adults.

The Art of Play

As a working artist, I've discovered that my own ability to play is an important component of my ability to create art. The element of playfulness that characterizes all creative investigations helps me generate new ideas and sustain the freedom necessary to plan and execute a work of art. The same can be said of children. Play brings out their individuality and allows their imaginations to thrive. All of my classroom lessons are introduced through play. This, I believe, is the most valuable teaching I can give.

When art instruction is planned around the experience of play, children can draw ideas from their own experiences instead of strictly following the teacher's lead, learning how to discover and plan for themselves. Playing requires no permanent commitment. Young artists can easily erase or change their work as they playfully sort through the possibilities. They have a chance to absorb each lesson, as well as to examine its premise and perhaps alter it, restate it, or even reject it. It is only through such personal exploration that original art can be born. Teaching art should never be reduced to the teacher's conception of what is good for children, what should be learned, and what should be communicated. As art teachers, we need to be less concerned about well-structured lessons and more concerned about giving our students the opportunity to express themselves. After all, the self is the most important ingredient in making art.

Emphasis on the value of children's play has a long tradition in childhood education. Friedrich Froebel (1782–1852), a German philosopher and educator called the father of the kindergarten, placed a great deal of importance on children's play. He believed that children developed knowledge by being encouraged to explore, to express themselves, and to learn by doing. Maria Montessori (1870–1952), whose influence is still acknowledged in the field of early childhood education, also stressed the importance of sensory play activities and developed her Montessori system based on this critical relationship.

Perhaps the greatest contemporary influence on the curricula of early education was Jean Piaget (1896–1980), the Swiss psychologist and philosopher. Basing his research on the theory that the only way for a child to develop intelligence is to construct it for him- or herself, Piaget concluded that early play experiences with concrete objects play a crucial role in cognitive development. Piaget was speaking directly to educators when he wrote: "Let us, therefore, try to create in the school a place where individual experimentation and reflection, carried out in common, come to each other's aid and balance one another" (1932, p. 404).

Although many of today's educators are willing to accept play as a part of preschool learning styles and people talk about the importance of play and its relationship to learning, many do not really respect the act of play or consider it a learning process. Too many subscribe to the belief that work is good and play is frivolous. As a result, the time for play is forever shrinking. But to children, play is serious business. Through play, they express what they know, clarify concepts, and organize their knowledge. D. W. Winnicott writes, "It is playing and only in playing that the individual child or adult is able to be creative and to use the whole personality, and it is only in being creative that the individual discovers the self" (1974, p. 189). In his book, *Running for Life*, George Sheehan tells us, "Play is the path to self-knowledge, the way to self-acceptance. If you would know yourself and then accept that knowledge, you must learn to play" (1980, p. 8).

As our world continues to shrink, more and more research scientists agree that the flexibility and creativity "developed in the context of play" will be just as important in the twenty-first century as the present day's basic skills (Almy M., 1984, p. 18). In 1988, the Association for Childhood Education International echoed this position in a paper promoting play as "essential to the healthy development of children from infancy through adolescence":

> As today's children move into the 21st century and continue to experience pressure to succeed in all areas of life, the necessity for play becomes more critical. ACEI supports those adults who respect and understand the power of play in children's lives. . . . These beliefs are rooted in research, theory

and exemplary practice. . . . ACEI also believes that teachers must take the lead in articulating the need for play in children's lives, including the curriculum. (138)

If play is to be an essential component of the school curriculum, the art class is a logical place for it. A playful attitude is the perfect frame of mind for the experimental ventures that art requires. Art lessons should be active experiences, journeys of the body and mind to fantasies reaching far beyond the classroom. These fanciful journeys into the imagination serve not only as means of self-expression but as ways to resolve some of life's mysteries. Dr. Olive Francks (1977, 191) says children's discoveries in art help them define the universe and structure their thinking in a visual way. Their art is important not so much for the finished product but for the mediation it provides between their inner and outer worlds.

If art is to have value as a means of expression, children must be encouraged to use the medium in their own way. Yet most early art experiences consist of copying someone else's patterns. In a 1989 article, "Whose Creation Is It, Anyway?" Professor Joan Moyer told this story:

> A seasoned art teacher was arranging her classroom for Open House. One wall, labeled ART, was adorned with children's art—colored leaves on a brown tree to depict the fall season. Some children's work was not on the display, however. When questioned, the teacher replied, "Those children did not follow the directions. Their pictures did not turn out like the rest, so I can't display them. It would be embarrassing to their parents." (17)

Clearly, teachers must learn to recognize and praise the spontaneity of children's creative expression, teaching them to feel free to engage in their own searches for what art is and what it can be.

In *The Nursery School: Human Relations and Learning* (1980), Katherine Read said:

> Too many of us have had art as an avenue of expression blocked for us by the teaching we received at school or at home. We are convinced that we can't draw a straight line and nothing we can do will ever rate as a work of art. We could probably have drawn much better and could have found more pleasure in art had there been less attention on the product and more on the process. We must safeguard [children's] use of art as a means of self-expression and not deprive them of this opportunity to be creative.

My personal research has shown that, when play rather than art is emphasized in the classroom, there is less preoccupation with talent or fear of failure. Children feel comfortable about trying new ideas, thus gaining control of the creative process. Play gives them the license to explore and investigate without being tied to rules, regulations, and preconceived art ideas. Free to pursue their own creative visions, to plan and question their own works, and to investigate art techniques individually, children produce impressive original artworks. This, to me, is the goal of art teaching: to inspire children to behave like artists; to reveal to them that art comes from within themselves, not from the teacher.

The Importance of Environment

Each summer I paint the landscapes around Woodstock, New York. But, first, I play with the trees, rocks, and bushes, wrapping them and dressing them in various materials and fabrics. This preliminary period of play is part of my self-preparation—a pressure-reducing activity during which I sort, investigate, rehearse, and gather ideas for my creative work. It is my way of becoming part of the environment before recording my ideas on canvas. When an art teacher creates a playful classroom environment, students are inspired to similar explorations. The art process becomes an avenue for personal search and discovery and, perhaps most important, an opportunity to be surprised by something new. The teacher helps the students frame a new context for familiar activities. They soon learn to see everything around them as possible source for display, selection, or manipulation: a floor or a chair becomes a base, a wall a background, the room a space, and people simply objects within that space. Through their playful discovering, they have begun to view their environment with fresh eyes and, as artists, to work with the space and the objects in that environment.

The contemporary art teacher should be less concerned with teaching how art is made and more concerned with providing the experiences and inspirations from which art can be made. Children remember best what they discover on their own. They are constantly discovering new environments because they are always eager to explore new places. Whether on an outdoor walk or in a supermarket aisle, they are forever investigating and collecting. Their journeys involve all their senses. They touch, smell, and sometimes taste everything new that they see. When art classrooms become play settings, arranged by the teacher to encourage investigative journeys, the children's explorations and discoveries will be recreated in their art and celebrated later in their art as adults.

In my classroom, I set up environments daily for the students to explore. They are encouraged to arrange, build, and take apart, to wrap, tear, roll, stuff, and crush. They play with hoses, film, tape, pipes, clips, rubber bands, and potato chips. Their play may involve building, tearing down, digging, inflating, packaging, or melting. They are constantly reshaping, stacking, tying, balancing, and arranging the new objects I bring to the classroom. Remember, children do not require detailed explanations or instructions when introduced to a new play environment. Their interest and enthusiasm for the unusual, complex, or new provide all the direction they need.

Outdoor Play Collecting

The Selection of Materials

Adult artists are constantly finding new sources for making art. This freedom and willingness to make anything from anything is an important artistic trait, and children do it best. "Let's build a bus" or "let's make dinner" means "let's invent it from materials we're playing with right now." Children may combine buttons, erasers, and pencil shavings to make a meal because, to a child, anything has the possibility of becoming anything else! But children need also to understand that, just as they can play with anything that is around, anything they play with can be used to create art. And if art is to deal with invention, tools and materials are needed for that invention. Through exposure to a wide range of materials, surfaces, and objects for art making, students will come to consider art media and processes in the broadest terms.

Playing with objects is the artist's way of testing and exploring new ideas. When asked about the inspiration for his creations, sculptor Henry Moore said, "The variety of objects in my studio provides me with many new ideas, simply by looking at and handling them. This might not happen if each object was in isolation" (1968, p. 502). Often, the objects themselves create a situation in which children can create and also, as Piaget said, discover structures and principles that make up their environment. For example, when young children play with puzzles and blocks, they are learning spatial concepts. Filling cups, pans, and cans with sand or water helps develop a sense of volume. Using large blocks and such to outline roads or build buildings introduces new orders, patterns, and relationships to the child players.

Students can be taught the accepted way of handling something, but it is even better if they come to understand the material or technique through play. Playing with a variety of materials simultaneously demonstrates traditional practices in art and calls them into question. Well-designed, creative games can help young artists not only learn more about a familiar material but rediscover it with fresh insight. To find out what a canvas is, for example, we may suggest the children fly it, stretch it, stuff it, or wear it; we may want them to look at different cloths, try various drapings, and examine a multitude of surfaces before they choose their particular canvas.

The internationally known Mummenschanz Players are an excellent example of artists who use the ordinary to create the extraordinary. They describe their creations this way:

> We find inspiration anywhere. If Bernie spots a roll of synthetic on the side of the road, he brakes, and gets out of the car to inspect it . . . Our loft is a laboratory of imagination where new "monsters" are created. We manipulate things . . . There is an irresistible urge to detour modern materials and change their functions. (Bohrer 1984, 56)

The manipulation of almost any object prepares the artist, mentally and physically, for the artwork itself. When children create art by displaying, rearranging, and playing with familiar objects, they begin to experience the personal value that art can have for them. As a teacher, I put as much stress on the activities that promote inner exploration and experimentation with art materials as I do on the physical work that results in a finished piece. To the artist, adult or child, the quest is every bit as important and exciting as the various endings expressed in an art work.

The Role of Movement in the Art Classroom

Children's art has little to do with still life but much to do with movement—especially moving bodies. When I watch the leaps, jumps, and poses of children in the midst of active play, I am convinced that their enthusiastic expression would be the envy of any contemporary choreographer.

Children's explorations of the space around them, and the experience of being in the center of that space, help them to understand the notion of space as a function of art. A young artist playing in three dimensions can learn something about the experience of working with art in two dimensions. In the context of their own movements through space, students can examine developmental stages in drawing, from the line to the circle, and begin to identify the relationship of the marks they may leave on an art surface.

Children should be encouraged to see the relationship between their play and their art. Covering a cake with icing may make them think of spreading paint over a surface; squeezing catsup onto a hamburger may remind them of how their hands and arms move when they draw on a page. Make-believe walks on paper, impersonations of animals, machines, or even alien creatures accompanied by markings with hands, fingers, feet, or the entire body can be seen properly as art or, at least, as a prelude to art.

If students become aware of the movements that are used in making art and of their own unique movement styles, they gain control over materials and tools and are better able to plan their works. They also learn that materials and tools suggest the kinds of movement with which they can be used. If movement play, rather than practice in traditional techniques, is stressed in art class, students develop a sense of freedom to mark all sorts of surfaces and alter forms in any way.

Freedom of movement is essential for an artist; it generates the independence of spirit so necessary for creativity to flourish. Our movements emanate from our personal rhythms: the sounds and music within us. Children sitting at desks are restricted in their movements; but move an art class from desktop to the floor, and watch how quickly kids regain the rhythm, joy, and grace of their playful selves.

Teachers can guide students' explorations through activities ancillary to free movement. The beat of a metronome, the music of a synthesizer, hands clapping, magic tricks, juggling—these are all acceptable activities for an art class. Incorporating jump ropes, balls, and Slinkys into teaching encourages students to recapture spontaneous movement. They should be permitted to move freely all around the room. And, as much as possible, everything else within the room should be movable, too—including the teacher. The teacher who passes freely through space, who jumps in the air or gets down on the floor, demonstrates a willingness to try new things and serves as an inspiration to the students to do likewise.

The teacher's role is to help the student view these activities within a new context, one that will help them handle art materials creatively and see movements within their environment in new and interesting ways. When these child-artists recognize the artistic possibilities in their everyday movements, they are encouraged to discover and create movements on their own, which intensifies their awareness of the concept of movement in art.

The Role of Performance in Art Class

"Watch me!" is a common plea of all children, often addressed to parents and teachers who are too busy or too tired to respond. Most children are natural performers who love to dress up and create their own dance or theater pieces. They build their performance stages anywhere and everywhere: on a stairway landing, in a doorway, in front of a fireplace. Their performances range from stand-up comedies to soap operas to renditions of their favorite popular songs. When they themselves aren't the stars, kids move Barbies, G.I. Joes, or favorite pets onto their make-believe stages.

Most children are experts when it comes to clowning and enjoy clowning in school. And while comic routines, crazy faces, and magic acts are not tolerated in a traditional classroom, they can become a viable part of the curriculum in art class. We say we want to uncover children's talent, but talent is too often confused with a child's ability to follow adult art instruction. Children are asked to become audiences instead of participants in their artistic lives. Too often their originality is squashed and their performances put on hold. In my art classes, I have watched these performances evolve into sources for their art. For a child, performance can be a prelude for art making, an opportunity for using a child's natural learning style. The fantasy life of children depends not just on memories but on an active search, a willingness to make everything they come in contact with, move, pose, or talk. My experience has shown that when children are allowed to bring inanimate objects to life or to assume new identities themselves, these new characters invariably become subjects of their artworks.

I believe performances are the sounds of art making. When children perform, they explore ideas though their bodies and their actions. In costume, or behind a mask, kids who normally may be repressed come alive and move more freely. Ideas become fanciful, and thoughts that may not be shared in everyday actions or even in drawings become accessible. Pretending gives children a sense of power to change things. And, in preparing to be someone or something else, they search for different tools and techniques to interact with. Eventually, the visual qualities of their play designs—the objects, the moves, the attitudes—become images on paper. I'm reminded of Paul Klee's essay "Creative Confessions," where he said, "Art does not reproduce the visible; it renders visible" (1967, p. 105).

Performing in the classroom also allows children to learn how to explain, show, and even defend their creative work and ideas in public. It's no surprise that kids are each others' best audiences—and most vocal critics. As a result, many play-art ideas actually develop from the challenge of others—from their input and questions. When children perform in class, those willing to try new things may risk more when they turn to art.

When kids have the chance to perform and be creative in front of their peers, they develop a better understanding not only of others but also of themselves. As they shape their dramatizations and make decisions as to form, materials, and style, they learn to appreciate the challenge and excitement of the creative process itself (Mandelbaum 1987, 186). Additionally, they learn emotional control as they take into account viewpoints that differ from their own (Fein 1986, vii–ix).

In a traditional classroom, children perform for a teacher who gives them instructions. The teacher in an art classroom, however, should be willing to perform for as well as with the students. A teacher's ability to accept the fantastic, say the ridiculous, and think the unbelievable can set the stage for children's inherent desire to perform. Teachers should make a special effort to surprise the class, in ways as simple as varying the pitch of the voice or punctuating their remarks with sound effects. They should attract double takes by doing such things as wearing a chef's hat while mixing paint in a blender. Even routine activities such as taking attendance, putting up signs, and distributing messages can be approached as a performance. When children observe an adult who is willing to perform for them, they begin to feel that there is nothing silly or childish in their own performances. A teacher's playfulness can shock them out of their traditional modes of thinking, allowing them to explore states of mind or actions more conducive to the art task.

The teacher can foster an attitude of performance at the beginning of an art lesson by establishing an imaginative or make-believe atmosphere. The room may be set up as a circus, a dance hall, or a cave. Just telling children to use their imaginations is rarely enough. Performance experiences need to be built into the lesson. When teachers are willing to deviate from normal teaching postures, they cultivate students who look forward to class and are stimulated to be creative in their own right.

Conclusion

In a post-performance conversation I once had with an accomplished saxophone player, the musician's response to my accolades was, "It was fun, man!" Artists, creative people in any media, often feel this way after performing creatively. They may feel tired, or even self-critical, but they will, nevertheless, feel that "it was fun!"

Art teaching should strive to capture the fun. Having fun is a prime motivation for making art. In order to maintain any creative effort for a long period, a sense of joy—fun, if you will—is necessary. When children play, they are having fun. They are free in their movements and in their thoughts. This is the perfect state of mind for the artist.

The act of playing is less burdened with pretensions, traditions, and preconceived ideas than any other human activity. Free of these constraints, we can tap the freshest source an artist can have—the clear spring of creativity in us all. In art, play is the experimental part of the process, the portion that frames ideas and rehearses them. In short, play expands our notion of what art is. Through play, child-artists learn to value their own ideas about art and find pleasure in the search. This is the difference between art that is taught and that personal art that is discovered through play.

Art is neither mysterious, nor the domain of the gifted, to be revealed by a select few and appreciated by a few others. In fact, I often tell my students that I don't know what art is but that the challenge of the artistic life is to find out the answer for oneself. And the possibilities for art are everywhere. The artistic life need not be a thing apart from the home, separate from our daily lives and everyday objects. Loading the refrigerator, cutting the grass, or setting the table all can be done playfully and artistically.

School art today tends to skip over or minimize the child's personal experiences in favor of the collective experiences of established artists or those of the art teacher alone. The emphasis is on teaching skills; the inspiration will come later. But, it often takes a lifetime of formal training to appreciate the beginnings of artistic consciousness: the beauty and inventiveness of creative play.

Throughout the rest of this book, I will share the basic assumptions and tenets underlying my approach to art education at the primary and secondary level. I will also suggest many classroom activities and teaching techniques that will help you create a classroom environment full of challenging visual, tactile, and media experiences that will free your students to invent their own creative visions.

My philosophy regarding the relationship between play and art is the result of more than sixteen years of teaching, my experiences with my own art, and the teaching experiments that my graduate students and I have made together in the public schools. It is based on the following premises:

- All children are artists, born with the natural ability to observe, formulate art ideas, and execute works of art on their own. For the young child, play and art are inseparable, and the longer this relationship lasts, the better individual creativity can be pursued.

- When we offer children a playful environment, their excitement about their own ideas, sensations, and feelings will stimulate them to make art.

- Children's art experiences should deal with the qualities of real materials within their environment rather than techniques for creating illusions of real things.

- Great art depends on movements emanating from both mind and body. Freedom of movement is essential in the art classroom because it generates the independent attitudes so necessary for the artist.

- Children's performances in play are vital to the performance of making art. They provide the inspiration for the child-artist to explore new movements, media, and subjects for expression.

- Art teaching is a celebration of the freedom to search for the artistic spirit in every person. The art teacher is the catalyst whose primary function is to create conditions within which children are inspired with their own ideas for making art.

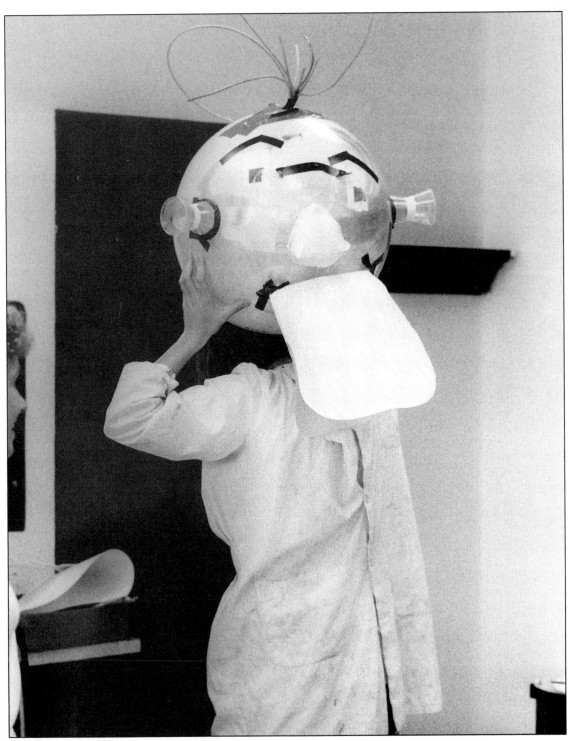

"Big Head" Rehearsals

Creating a Classroom Environment for Art

"I don't know who discovered water but I'm sure it was not a fish." (McLuhan, 1984)

As an artist, I start each new day, each new project, as a search for meaning. This is what we want to foster in our students, future artists, and meaning makers. I don't expect my art to come from the observations and experiences of others, and I don't expect my students to make art that way either. Learning art from a traditionally prepared art lesson makes no more sense than does making art by copying the work of others. Art is original, not imitative. So, although occasionally copying the works of others can supplement artists' needs and ideas, learning the right technique, following the correct procedure, can be self-defeating. Art is a personal act, and children should be allowed to capitalize on unique, yet universal, experiences instead of being inundated with design formulas unique only to their originators. Children's art does not derive from a dialogue with the world of adult artists, but rather from their own discoveries of space, color, and symmetry. Play experiments suggest a searching notion of design learned from experiments and derived from individuals. In other words, playing teaches students how to take charge of an art search, to look toward themselves as inventors, and feel the stirrings of great voices and powers within.

Playfulness is inhibited when students feel that art comes from someone else. Even young children lose track of their visions and capabilities to seek new ideas when overwhelmed by teachers and artists. Students should learn art with a teacher, not only from a teacher. Artists and children have to feel that they have unique ideas and sense that an ability to play is a lifelong medium of endless discovery.

If students are to make art that goes beyond the boundaries normally defined by school art, they must be encouraged to step outside of the school environment. Since it is not always possible to do this physically, they must acquire the skills to do it imaginatively. Teachers can foster this by actually taking students outside the classroom or by constantly re-creating the classroom itself. By rearranging the physical environment in the classroom—agitating, reshuffling, and redesigning it—we are able to inspire the imagination and thinking, in ourselves and in our students.

The Limitations of a Conventional Art Classroom

A traditional art classroom looks like any other classroom in a school. Designed for the convenience of the teacher and the school administration, it is set up to promote maximum order and efficiency. Traditional rows of tables and desks evoke a closed grid more than an open canvas. Furnishings act as barriers to movement. Walls display announcements or serve as the one place where student art is acceptable. The teacher is the center of attention, bringing in and handing out art materials, which are usually delivered to students who remain in their seats. Every movement is predictable, routine; no unexpected changes disrupt the environment. Art lessons are preshaped, messes are cleaned up, and every object has its place. If something is moved, it is expected to be returned to its original spot. A room that has changed from the way it was previously set up is considered a room in disarray.

And what about art? Art is made at a table where the student sits. Nothing else in the room has any relevance except what is directly in front of the student. Art making is expected to be inspired through words—the teacher's words—and not action. Creativity is expected to originate inside the student's head, rather than from multiple stimuli from the external world—in this case, the classroom environment.

The Possibilities of the Art Classroom

Art classrooms should be significantly different from other classrooms where students sit and listen. Teachers should visualize the art room as a three-dimensional canvas where multiple planes can be orchestrated for an infinite variety of sensory effects. Art rooms should be discovery spaces, not lecture halls; the room should be designed as a place where students come together to *find* art, not hear about it. The best art classroom is conceived as a playroom, a place that draws students out of their seats and encourages them to dream and fantasize. It should allow for temporary constructions that can be easily disassembled and replaced. Students should be invited to touch, move, construct, try on, and try out the things around them. They should be urged to alter and gain control of the space around them in order to control the play and art within them and ultimately to act on their own ideas.

Outside the classroom, children turn to the environment freely, continually discovering great ideas on their own. They create in snow, in a toolshed, a dollhouse, or at the beach. They find new spaces, new materials, and new tools all around them. An art room should strive to re-create the atmosphere of a child's own room, a playground, or a sandy beach—the spaces that promote playfulness and creativity.

Children should find in the classroom their own artist's studio. Just as artists come to their studios having culled observations and ideas from elsewhere, from anywhere, and often work surrounded by physical reminders of these ideas, so students should be encouraged to bring their own ideas and objects from outside into the school art classroom. These environmental finds are a superior source of inspiration to students. They should fill the shelves, tabletops, desks, and even floors of the classroom, creating a playful atmosphere and promoting fresh thinking and creativity.

The classroom environment should itself be considered student art, an important medium through which ideas can be created, presented, and shared. Galleries and exhibition spaces inspire artists to learn about their own work by observing the work of their colleagues. The art classroom can be not one but many spaces within which to display the originality of many minds. One large classroom can include a private studio for solitary work, a gallery for showing work, and an ever-changing environment for student-artists to explore and exhibit new finds.

An art room, above all, needs to be a *fun* environment, open and flexible and able to accommodate the various needs of many individual creative minds that will feed and inspire one another. It should be fundamentally a place of choices.

The Liberation of the Classroom

The tools of art no longer live only in the art supply store. Artists now shop everywhere in the environment for the inspiration and means to make art. They must be willing to search the environment, think about what they see or find in it, and respond to it.

Classroom environments may be carefully designed by the teacher, or they may contain only clues and raw materials for students to use to begin or complete the setup. Regardless of the originator, it should be possible to alter and re-alter any environment, as well as to elaborate upon it during classroom play sessions.

The Importance of Memory: Past and Future

When we tie an art environment to a student's own fantasies and memories, we relay a message about the rich resources within each individual's past. Remember playing house? Building castles at the beach? Digging in a sandbox? Going to the zoo?

An environment need not look exactly like a beach or a zoo or a house for it to recapture the feeling of the experience and validate the importance of each student's own life story as an event from which to draw or make meaning. It may be altered slowly throughout the class period, its design changing over several stages of play. Photographs, sketches, and audio and visual recordings, as well as smaller-scale re-creations or reproductions, are all possible ways to

Ana's Room: Play Setups in Home Environments

preserve, protect, or recapture the memory of an environment found to be particularly inspiring or exciting. Even after it has been changed, covered, or disassembled, memories of a classroom environment can remain valuable sources on which a student may be able to draw at unexpected moments.

The Importance of Observation

Let's not worry about the limitations of our school space—the things we *cannot* do in them. Let us think of its advantages and unique features and detail which features would be best for what kinds of play.

Before making even minor changes, observe the classroom carefully. Look for special openings, closets, unusual corners, or views. Don't be overwhelmed by the challenge of creating new paths, divisions, and arrangements. Instead, think flexibly about the space, and search for possibilities in sculpting, shaping, dividing, or partitioning it. Think about play activities where students stay close to the floor and those that might allow them to move to different levels (whoever said desks were not for standing on?). Check out the various views from the door as you enter the room. Look at all corners and at every window. Notice how the light changes during the day and how this affects the room's existing patterns and surfaces.

How we enter a room, where we sit, what we look at in its design and details can change our experience and idea of that room. Instead of feeling controlled and manipulated by the spaces around us, we can assert our right to enter a playful space—playfully! Students should be motivated to become interested in the spaces around them and seek out ideas and clues there for their art.

The Importance of the New

Creating something new out of something old, turning the familiar into the exotic, is a way of keeping our minds and our senses awake. Think of the art room in new ways: as a stage, an airport runway, a swimming pool, a rehearsal studio, or a throne room in a palace. Making room for a ski run, a hula hoop contest, or a plane landing helps students visualize new environmental shapes and possible alterations.

Free space visualization also helps teachers talk to students about the concept of space. For example, when visualizing a theatrical environment, we must consider alterations in lighting, possible influences for sound effects, designs for entrances and exits, and movement of furniture to allow the unhindered crossing of the theater's players.

The Element of Surprise

Students are surprised to be able to play in school. They are surprised to see toys in school and surprised that play objects have anything to do with art. Students are surprised when their teacher is interested in the things they are interested in. They are surprised when they learn that the classroom is not a classroom today but a fish tank, a color store, a shape warehouse, and so on. The classroom environment is the gateway to all these surprises. It is the surprises incorporated into each art lesson that demonstrate the essence of art—that is, daring the extraordinary, searching for the personal, seizing the opportunity to be different.

Imaginative Re-Creation of Objects

Each detail in a classroom can become many things in a "let's pretend" environment. A light switch can activate a robot's performance, a time machine, or a light show. A chair can be a barber's chair, a rocker, or a throne. A closet can be an elevator, a secret vault, or a magician's prop chamber. A floor can be a checkered game board or a parking lot. Class windows may look out of an airport control tower or be an observatory to the heavens.

With makeup, alterations, coverings, and new signs, each environment can assume a new identity, changing the feeling of the room and its surfaces and open the door to creative thinking about art tools and surfaces.

The Power of Naming

A new name for a space can evoke a new vision of it. Call the art room a test kitchen, a space laboratory, or a discovery room. The use of signs, verbal signals (like "Sshh!" You'll wake the baby!"), or guided suggestions ("Watch your step on that escalator!") can create interest, arouse curiosity, alter expectations, or build suspense.

The Availability of a Space for Solitary Work

A school art classroom should be able to accommodate students who want to work alone or independently for periods at a time. Like artists, children at play may talk to themselves, daydream, stare off into space, or move in fits and starts as they develop the course of their personal investigation. Students who separate themselves from the group are often taking the first step toward making original artwork. Such departures should be encouraged, and each classroom should be designed with some area for personal space and art adventures.

Special Environments in the Classroom

The classroom environment should be a place filled with surprises and unusual objects. Special events should inspire playfulness and creativity as students interact with and test out the environmental offerings. By creating alternative environments and challenging our students to respond spontaneously to them, we are teaching our students to look for an art lesson, instead of being handed one—to seek art materials, techniques, tools, and subject matter *everywhere*. This is the beginning of learning to welcome and celebrate the new.

I once began a semester by taking students on a trip to a major toy store in the area. Teachers who accompanied us were asked to study the expressions of the children and notice their excited behavior. As we moved through the store, discovering soap crayons, toy typewriters, magic slates, confetti, and Legos, it became obvious how each item could evoke a fantasy that could lead, in turn, to a new art theme, technique, construction, or playful setup.

Adults and children alike come alive in a toystore. Our eyes dart around, visually excited by all the shapes, colors, sizes. Our hands reach out to feel, caress, try out. We play with a joystick and dream beyond it, visualizing the remote control of an unusual form in space; we try out a laser gun and imagine drawing laser images; stuffed animals give way to images of soft sculpture; party accessories inspire ideas for gatherings and celebrations we have yet to experience. Each object suggests a new environment, an unusual event, or a unique play possibility.

The art room today should model itself after the toy store—an open art market where all elements are available and open to experimentation. Everything in the art room can and should become a possible art tool, art surface, or art medium.

The art room should also be a satellite location for students' home environment. Carpets, foam, or gravel can be used to recreate home floor spaces, and students may be encouraged to walk barefoot—itself a trademark of the comforts of home playing. Lacking the many interesting storage spaces found in the home, we need to use a variety of portable containers to invite browsing shoppers or to set up various school displays. Instead of the many home lighting setups, we need to bring in portable lights, from flashlights to projectors, to increase the "playability" of school lighting. To enrich the furnishings of the normal school classroom, students can be asked to bring in fluffy pillows, throw rugs, chairs from home. They should also be encouraged to bring in their collections and personal discoveries. Marbles, buttons, appliance knobs, and handles brought to school by teachers and students alike make the classroom a place full of exciting "stuff." Discoveries can be made anywhere in a classroom like this: in a school desk, a container, a windowsill. Anyone may plant a surprise. Think how the mystery of finding an unusual object on the floor could suddenly illuminate a vast floor environment—never noticed before!

The way an environment is introduced—the context created—can also influence students' perceptions of their surroundings. An ordinary simple setting can be made extraordinary by a creative "showing" of the place. Instructions such as "watch where you step" or a teacher who tiptoes over an unseen "obstacle" can set up offbeat and unexpected explanations, which students can share with one another or muse on privately.

Environmental journeys can be planned with varying degrees of detail—from a ride through a room (on an elephant made of students?), to a treasure hunt (complete with maps and prepared clues). Students can be asked to play fortune seekers, explorers, or wizards—or to come up with their own roles.

"Plays" can take place inside a big coat, a closet, under an umbrella, in a tent, or in a box. Ideas for such space "designs" come easily from observation of children's natural play activity.

The art room can become an environment that enables students to enjoy fantasy travel. Set up secret doors or passages, elevators, time machines, tunnels, trap doors, or dressing rooms. The room can itself be a vehicle, lined with carpets, rearranged seats or tables, taking students on rides to still other environments.

The introduction of a unique color, unusual form, or unexpected substance can have a major impact on space. Inexpensive props such as Day-Glo rubber bands, colorful candies, paper clips, or potato chips may be considered in environmental "placements."

Viewing a room from an unusual angle or height or looking at an ordinary item in a not-so-ordinary way can excite the imagination. So can following a trail of clues to hidden "treasure." Objects brought in from the outdoors—a bird's nest or jar of worms—can have an unexpected effect, while certain technologies—slide projectors, tape recorders, audio and video equipment—can greatly enhance excitement in a relatively simple classroom setting. And some environmental settings can be brought to life with flashlights, confetti, juggling, dances, and the performance of magic.

By trial and error, you can learn to visualize different play environments—the shapes of them, the entrance paths, the ways students might move or play in them, and the details of object selection, placement, packaging, and display. The use of interesting wrappings, supports, stands, markings, and signs can all make a vast difference in how students view their art spaces. However, it is important to keep in mind that the environment is never solely responsible for creative activity; rather, the vision, personal experiences, and spontaneous performances of the students brings to life the environment—which then acts to animate and inspire the student.

The Psychological Environment

The Importance of Beauty

We don't want to fill the room with just any old junk. The classroom—originally designed for utility alone—cries out for beauty; as artists, student and teacher alike, we must take special care to select colorful, exciting, inspiring-to-look-at additions to the everyday classroom environment. Students soon learn to think of their classroom as a place that needs constant maintenance and replenishment—much as a garden needs the loving attention of its caretaker. As students nourish the environment around them, the environment will directly nourish their spirits in return.

User Friendliness in the Classroom

Friendliness to found objects, fearlessness of clutter, and openness to children's tastes and values—even if they differ from those of traditional art—all create the proper psychological environment for art to be born. When students respond playfully to a room—examining it, touching it, setting things up in it—they are learning that the environment is accessible to them. If they feel free to play in the school art environment, they can begin to move beyond normal boundaries, beyond school assignments, to uncover their own ideas and art. Art environments in the classroom, therefore, should be touchable, huggable, stackable. Students should be able and permitted to interact with the environment using all their senses.

The Freedom to Choose

When designing environments, the question of space choices is a primary consideration. Where should we set up a highway or railway of tracks? Where best to set sail on a make-believe ocean? Each space should be analyzed for its particular qualities and its potential to support specific play ideas. As students learn about choosing, they are training their eyes to be ever alert, playfully searching. They should begin with a wide-open outlook, but they need to keep small details in mind as well—an unusual doorknob, wall hanger, or water fountain might inspire a student to creativity as much as a more apparently impressive feature of the environment.

The Influence of Mood

Environmental design is really a multimedia art form that may use extraordinary and ordinary objects in playful ways. Such diverse materials as snow, brussel sprouts, caterpillars, or tree branches may suggest play ideas and stimulate students' fantasies. A display of bright yellow pencils placed in geometric patterns on the floor can suggest a construction site. A row of marshmallows, the sound of marbles in special containers invite playful attention—the possibility of tasting or touching. All sorts of inventions can create, alter, or suggest a mood. Less direct stimuli—an invitation to a special event or the adventure of burrowing for a prize inside a cereal box—can also excite the imagination. The teacher may devise an environment or event, or one group of students may initiate something for another's response.

The Teacher's Role

Every semester, before the first play class, I nervously pace the hallways. First classes are nerve-racking but extremely important for setting a playful tone and differentiating the art class from all the others. It helps to know that it will take only a few minutes to feel comfortable and that the initial investment will return dividends all year. Excitement is contagious, and in the presence of excited players even shy teachers gain courage. "To think about starting," one teacher in our program attests, "can be difficult, but it is easier than one would imagine since children quickly get the message of fun and eagerly join us." A relaxed, informal, and involved class resulting from play situations makes initial jitters quickly subside.

Not being fully in control or able to predict every step of a lesson feels risky at the start. It *is* risky—until you relax. Explorations feel scary because we're venturing into previously uncharted territory, foreign to our notions of how things are supposed to be in school. We fear that kids will feel too inhibited to respond at the beginning, and we worry that some colleagues will disapprove of what we're doing. But most children, however shy, will quickly be drawn in by the rest of the class, while our colleagues, at least, have thought that what we have done was wonderful. And if being the star who initiates and orchestrates is too intimidating, pressures can be somewhat reduced by taking one of the supporting roles, leaving the leading role to a student.

Parting with the routine setups and responses of a school day while courting momentary embarrassments and risks becomes easier when we consider that such play would be quite natural outside and at home; it only seems awkward because it is taking place in a classroom. As teaching begins to feel more like an artistic act, it also begins to feel right for an artist-teacher. "Playing," said one teacher, "is not only more fun than lecturing, but it requires the most creative thoughts I have." Teachers report feeling more artistic in play classes and seeing kids become more naturally inventive. As we relinquish our teacherly roles and traditional behaviors, we will discover a vast variety of new roles and productive relationships that will more effectively induce children's creative responses, thereby achieving our raison d'être.

A teacher's experimental and innovative spirit can make its mark on every aspect of the environment, whether students receive strange objects when they ask for a hall pass or must submit to purple fingerprinting when attendance is taken. Everything the teacher brings or adds to the environment can be extraordinary. She can be a producer, director, and performer in it; she can fill it with surprises, visual pleasures, and fun-filled directives. Students should feel that anything can happen.

A teacher's willingness to take part in activities—to test-fly a space craft, get down on the floor, stand up on a chair—testifies to the acceptability of playing in class. The teacher is telling students that it is, indeed, okay. They are quick to catch on; they will follow the teacher's lead.

The art teacher need not give up the notion of communicating ideas normally taught in a traditional art program. But these ideas will inevitably have more meaning if they are grounded in the students' own participation and experienced directly in a living, dynamic environment. The role of the art teacher should be to inspire, not to tell; the environment is the true teacher, the teacher its instrument and shaper.

Model Environments

Discovery Environments

- On a plot of grass (model-railroading turf) and over rough terrains (rugs and blankets), we pile up rocks and pebbles in art class. Brought in from outdoor play, the largest stones are wrapped in newspaper bearing red "Handle with Care" labels. Leaves, pine cones, flowers, and even a butterfly are pressed under the stones. Only a bird's song (on tape) breaks the silence of the forest (art room).

- I enter the room pulling a chain of shiny red wagons loaded with all shapes and sizes of old luggage, each piece secured by chains and locks that make them look like traveling vaults. Interest piqued, students need little encouragement to browse, lifting, shaking, pulling, or quietly listening to the ticking clues inside. But before the grand opening of the sticky old locks, students privately weigh the merits of shiny silver trays, a collection of old work gloves, and shopping baskets available to help them carry whatever treasures may lie hidden in containers.

- Armed with plastic shovels, safari hats, and containers labeled "for specimens only," students embark on a discovery walk. In the schoolyard, they encounter small, flagged markers designating excavation mounds and other sites for possible digging. I report that these marked sites had been pretested with computerized devices and found to contain the bones and treasures now on display. After much discussion of probabilities and possibilities, my crew and I proceed to nearby velvet cloths whereon lie some puzzling artifacts marked in chalk with numbers telling where they were found. We are further intrigued by the red prodding rods available at the site that are said to attract mysterious forces buried beneath the sand.

The art classroom can become a stand-in for the many interesting places outside its walls. Every tiny square on a floor or ceiling can be dressed, designed, or even lifted to reveal surprising clues. As teachers, we're licensed to bring in all sorts of props from home—objects to lift; openings to unzip; things to unwrap, take apart, move, or look into. Such props are a necessary part of our plan to engage students' natural curiosity and creativity, inspiring them to experience new environments. You might even lay out the environment ahead of time in a drawing that envisions what the room should look like and how objects can be most interestingly or mysteriously placed. Your creative use of space can inspire students to do the same.

Performance Environments

+ Three brightly colored hula hoops lie on the floor. An old theatrical fixture projects light into each circle. Next to the three-ring stage, in semidarkness, are festively wrapped crates. An expectant audience fills chairs encircling the stage. "Unfolding the Greatest Act" reads the label on one box containing a selection of old folding yardsticks. Inside the "hanger jugglers" crate is a variety of colorful plastic clothes hangers. Fresh, white Ping-Pong balls fill the third container. With soft circus sounds and recorded laugh tracks in the background, tension builds as we await our student performers and actors, who are invited to wrap themselves in miles of rulers, balance scores of hanger configurations, and juggle Ping-Pong balls and popcorn. An old "Applause" sign redly flickers on and off above the scene.

+ We attach balloons to a long runway constructed of every table in class. A play microphone awaits the announcer while we light the runway with flashlights. Some students are selecting the party noisemakers they will need for sound effects. An array of bicycle mirrors, truck mirrors, and many other kinds of mirrors glints next to a rack of costumes readied for our student stars. Closets soon become dressing rooms, as students finish browsing through jewelry cases, makeup boxes, and hat containers. Be patient . . . the show will begin in just a few minutes.

+ In rows of open lunch boxes, small plastic figures (including California Raisins) patiently wait to take their places on lunchbox stages with colorful napkin curtains and modern revolving sets made of paper plates.

One stagehand is attaching the microphone to a radio amplifier and setting it beside an area "For Sound Effects Staff Only." Other stagehands working backstage double-check to be sure that old fans, fish-tank motors, toy instruments, and noisemakers of all kinds are ready to support our stars on stage. Everybody, take your places . . . You're on!

Each lesson can take place on a different stage. Sheets, fabrics, paneling, and blankets can form dramatic backdrops, curtains, or tents for a performance area. Projection plays with slides, colored gels, or punctured slides can introduce new dimensions of color or points of light. Collections of funny glasses, fancy gloves, disguises of all kinds can be brought into class—in a variety of containers. Tiny creatures, dollhouse furnishings, soldiers, pull toys, and stuffed animals can participate in both toy-scale and full-scale performances.

Adventure Environments

♦ On a patchy pattern of silver and colored papers, a chair stands isolated in the middle of the room. Tiny hotels and little houses cover the ground, while open umbrellas spread their shade over several old backpacks labeled "parachutes." Wearing my large Jump Master pin on my pocket and shouting over the roar of a helicopter engine, I prepare students for their first solo parachute jump. Busy whispers ripple through the line of expectant paratroopers winding up to the actual jumpsite: "Look how little the houses are from here!"

♦ Now we wrap plastic around table legs to fashion large aquariums and put chairs together to support plastic sheeting that will shelter Day-Glo worms, shells, old sponges, and battered toy boats. Live goldfish in plastic bags hang over the see-through environments. At the entrance, we hang our diving gear—swim goggles and black plastic tubing—on plastic hooks, then check containers marked to indicate the depth of each dive. Every container has a red warning light. Surprising finds are placed in the tank to lure divers. Of course, underwater drawing tools cannot be ordinary: some have been wrapped in plastic; others housed in protective boxes with only their points exposed. Long rubber gloves with drawing tools taped to them are also available for undersea sketching. Ordinary paper would be useless, but divers can select from a bucketful of drawing surfaces—including tiles, foams, and plastics—that has been lowered into the tank.

♦ Chairs lie on the floor flat on their backs, tied together two by two with plastic tubes. We are ready to strap our astronauts into place—on *their* backs—with a collection of belts. Day-Glo blocks, shoelaces, and stickers dangle above and around us. As students blast off to a prepared flight tape, we dim the lights and watch our planets shine in the dark.

Each adventure environment has its own extraordinary conditions that require the use of different tools and surface treatments, just as changes in atmosphere, temperature, gravity, or pressure require a variable approach to the artwork. In each new environment, I emphasize to students that we are the first observes, players, and artists to experience it. When students think of themselves as the first underwater sculptors or as the first landscape artists to draw from a parachute, they take on the responsibility of exploring each move, each tool, each surface as no one ever has before them, creating new wrappings, adding weights, trying extension devices, and formulating unusual handles or means of manipulating tools. This is a way to break new art ground, and it is how artists must approach the world around them to make art.

Technology Environments

♦ Enter our class under a large NASA sign. We've set up our space drawing lab with a variety of low-tech apparatus to seek high-tech answers to art actions of the future. A stack of gloves near a child's pool invites us to engage in underwater drawing tests. We set two portable trampolines beneath floodlights to test orbital movements and weightlessness and add remote-controlled devices and robot arms to students' chairs. The latter become lunar rovers as we attach TV garage-door openers to serious-looking clipboards on which we record experiment ideas. In each corner of our lab, self-sealing plastic bags labeled "sterile" are ready to received whatever extraterrestial objects we will find outside. As flight preparation continues, we work in our tailoring corner to design space suits out of Legos, boxes, and foils. Our flight trainers may look like ordinary school trash cans but there are unusual objects aboard.

♦ Colorful giant disks point toward the heavens. Labeled with stickers that say "The Big Ear," garbage can covers, taped to the backs of chairs, are tuned to the universe, ready to transmit signals back to our student-players. Each unit is tied to a private listening station outfitted with students' Walkman headphones. Soon, giant television screens—white paper hung on walls—will broadcast pictures of the signals sent from other worlds that we could only listen for at first. Attached to our screens by suction cups and clips are bright telephone wires that lead to magnetic laser viewers made of sunglasses placed on control tower tables.

♦ A cardboard clock at the classroom entrance announces the time of the next show: 8:45 A.M. As students enter the planetarium, I loan them colored sunglasses. Looking through these skyviewers, they marvel at the planetarium ceiling lined with plastic and fabric samples. Projectors along the floor allow free light play on the ceiling or anywhere else, while rubber bands hold colored gels in front of each projector lens. Together, we prepare slides found in boxes labeled "star research units": using specially designed devices, we mark, scratch, and puncture the slides to allow a thousand light beams to flow through. Human hair, nail polish, stickers, or a bug can then help us view strange cracks and objects projected on distant planets.

♦ Today, our famous painting and drawing art robot is being wired for action. We fit classroom chairs with orange extension cords, fishing-rod arms, vacuum-tube hands, and joystick attachments. Some models we equip with wheels (using skateboards and roller skates), others with picturephones—toy telephones on Etch-a-Sketch bases. These units—the latest in robotics—will be controlled by classroom researchers who are also, it happens, experienced computer and video game players.

Kids' interest in X-ray vision, laser weapons, remote controls, robot arms, and star searching can translate into the tools, places, and special events that classroom plays are built upon. High tech can be explored through low tech: household items, Legos, colorful wires, antennae, switches, and motors can be converted to power imaginary vehicles, inventions, and actions. Through the use of such ordinary props, students are invited to use real or made-up technology terms, sometimes borrowed from familiar toys.

Through "technology" play environments created in the art room, we can learn to hear farther, see things smaller or larger, and dream of ideas secretly, openly, more outlandishly than anywhere else, perhaps even outdoing any practicing artist or scientist.

Party Environments

♦ Our creamy pink tent with party invitations and silver balloons taped to its flaps proves irresistible. A portable light adds color and warmth to the tent's entrance while confetti-filled clouds (see-through plastic packages) hover overhead, ready to burst when conditions are right. No one has trouble finding the event—festive stickers point the way. Toy soldiers and fierce animals (plastic or stuffed) guard the road. But the VIP they have been deployed to protect has already arrived—an oversized, flashy (Barbie) car parked outside our tent provides a clue to the guest of honor's identity.

♦ We're really busy today—excited, too—as we roll out red carpet for our royal guests. Formal wallpaper taped to a wall sets off a throne at the room's center. Place cards on the table—the duke of this or that, the princess of here or there—still need to be arranged; so do the dishes, the tablecloth, and the napkins in a variety of royal colors. Tables will soon be set with puffy makeup sponges, cotton balls, buttons, erasers and other desserts. Our world-famous baker is preparing to decorate and set before the royal family the largest cake ever seen—layers of softly wrapped classroom trash cans. Musicians are also busy, readying funnily shaped tubes through which to announce the big event.

Parties we have had, parties we wish or dream for, can all come true in the art room—occasions to dress up, wrap beautiful packages, and invite our favorite characters to share in some fun. Whether it is an environmental design fit for a king or just a small intimate get-together, a party can be a challenge to the creative spirit of classroom players, inspiring student art with the particular quality of joyfulness and playfulness that parties nurture best and most fully.

Store Environments

♦ My sweatshirt reads "Born to Shop" and I'm arranging red "Sale" signs between new merchandise rolled out on tables. I've already set up classroom tables featuring tastefully arranged gloves, hair ornaments, and old-fashioned hats. In an adjacent setup, I've adorned white styrofoam heads with ribbons, hair pieces, and headbands. And, of course, two silver toy cash registers are ready for business—and just in time. Here come the shoppers!

Children love to shop, but unlike adult shoppers—who seek bargains, useful items, or status merchandise—kids shop much as an artist searches for materials. Their approach is freer, open to tactile seduction—a playful gathering of any and all interesting-looking objects, regardless of usefulness.

Any art classroom can become a store, an interesting place to browse through, try things on, show things off. The environment can have shelves, hangers, shopping carts, shopping bags, and wrapping materials. The moods of different kinds of stores can be set through color, lighting, signage, music, and/or mirrors. In planning the setup of a store, students experience the art of arrangement: how to showcase a collection of perfume bottles, candy, carrots, or pastry; how to draw attention to an unusual item for sale; or how to draw customers into their store. Students feel challenged to create new ways to get people to see and, in doing so, learn to see and select for themselves.

House Environments

♦ A room filled with colorful towels, wildly patterned beach blankets spread over beach chairs, with a sea of canvas-like roofed structures and partitions creates a typical beach or poolside house.

Displays in a Store Play

♦ A pile of books can become a mountain and forts; pillows can surround an island; a red wagon topped with a large box can become a trailer or covered wagon; a stack of funnels or a row of umbrellas suggests new ideas in contemporary building design. An empty fish tank can simulate a modern glass building.

Most rooms are arranged for children by their parents or their teachers. But just as the idea of transforming business lofts to residences appeals to adults, so children enjoy remodeling space to make room for their own collections, stuffed toys, or other friends. They explore the many views inside and outside their different neighborhoods as they decorate, receive mail, or drive by their new homes. Post-it pads, empty staple boxes, and puffy packing materials become sample floor coverings, wall treatments, or other home decorations. Pillows, blankets, and all manner of other items from home create three-dimensional—and later, two-dimensional—environments to play in and draw in.

Private Environments

- Neatly folded blankets of different colors and patterns are carefully placed on the classroom floor. Room lights are lowered, flashlights are readied, and students under blankets begin to make faces and explore drawings in their private studios. In these hideaways, flat wooden drawers contain all kinds of bicycle, car, and truck mirrors for face explorations. Hats, stickers, and disguises are also there, along with makeup, shaving cream, and soft papers for wrapping, tracing, rubbing, and massaging facial features. Drawing by flashlight, students learn about the face in privacy as they light it, feel it, and cover it while recording their impressions on Saran Wrap placed over the mirrors.

- As students come through the door, they can't see the room because clotheslines hung with fabrics and sheets block their view of the space within. Behind shiny surfaces, students make faces. Behind transparent plastic curtains, students play X-ray. From private aisles, students signal each other by making noises, sticking out hands and feet, gesturing with hand puppets, or whatever else comes to mind.

Art and play can benefit from secrecy and private surroundings. Being away from an audience can be an effective means to draw out self-conscious older players. Playing under tables and blankets, whispering in the dark, passing secret notes—these processes can foster a sense of mystery, unveiling, or even exposure—itself a part of the artist's experience. Private exhibition spaces can be created to display some artworks. Students love packages, presents, envelopes—the excitement of uncovering what's inside. Student plays may involve feeling, looking, or smelling inside secret curtains, openings, boxes, or keyholes to reveal the secrets therein.

Basic Environments

- To keep birds away from a freshly seeded garden, our neighbor planned to mulch with a bale of hay. Birds stayed away, but children didn't! Spreading fresh hay out on the sidewalk obviously was great fun, so I rushed down to buy my own bright yellow bundle for the next art class. Green plastic served as artificial turf, but that didn't make the straw any less inviting to spread with pitchforks from a recent McDonald's collection. To put our activity in perspective, I projected famous hayfield paintings (mostly from the Impressionists) on the white walls. But the kids' activity more resembled Jackson Pollock's as they dumped, tossed, and scattered their straw. Later, we tried the forks as brushes, which, along with straw clumps, were playfully repositioned, dropped, traced, and painted.

Play Homes Under the Table

- An orange "Caution" sign stands tall at the classroom entrance, and another sign says "Wet Floor." Students are invited to admire the lakes and streams of small water puddles, beside which are placed eye droppers, spoons, sponges, and other water-dispersing devices. The center of the room is draped in a raincoat, a soft plastic sheet with many wrinkles into which water can be channeled. Umbrellas are left open or closed to drip over the plastic and act as water feeders to the site. A container of ice is held ready to be placed on square floor tiles for us to observe its sculptural meltings. Bubble bath is available for spooning into wet spots or mixing with food colors. Finally, colored spotlights wait to light up the bubbles, foam, ice, and suds whipped up in all this water play.

- A sign posted on the classroom door proclaims this the world's largest sandbox, according to the Guinness Book of World Records. A large tape-marked area waits to be filled with tiny playthings. Boxed items and loosely formed mounds—of pencil shavings, fish-tank gravel, assorted candies on silver trays, cupcake tins, and colorful plastic tubs—are also on the floor. Mounds of crushed stones, loosely arranged shells, and colored earth all find a place in children's play pools, while shovels and pails, toy cranes, and bulldozers stand in work spaces around the room.

Sweepers we've constructed of chairs with brooms tied to them clear major paths.

♦ Almost invisible lines of plastic fishing line hang and sway from the ceiling, each weighed down by a differently shaped magnet. On the floor are metal objects individually placed or interestingly packaged—a collection of old keys (to mysterious places), fishing lures and sinkers, squiggly springs and Slinkys. A laundry line complete with pulleys, old clothespins in a black canvas bag, and piles of laundry in great colored fabrics are in a basket, ready to fly.

These settings may not have specific themes, but they offer interesting and familiar materials to play with on a variety of surfaces and in a variety of configurations. Each play expands the basics of all playing and art. In each setting, unusual and beautiful materials are presented in an inviting situation that requires little or no explanation.

Conclusions

What we ask students to do inside the art room may appear different from what they do in other school spaces, yet good teachers will encourage similar practices in other subjects. A classroom can divide, restrain, control—or it can bring together, free, inspire, and evoke curiosity and creativity. Teachers who are environmentally aware and sensitive can nurture the qualities that turn art students into independent thinkers, joyful people, and active creative artists.

Carousel Plays

Materials

— ◆ —

Now that we have established the importance of creating a living, dynamic environment where we use all our senses, let's zero in on the materials within that environment.

When students use a pencil or crayon in school, generally they do not experience any particular delight and excitement. Similarly, the paper on which they practice their penmanship or drawing is simply there. What were once the tools of invention become the tools of necessity as assignments pile up and the marking of surfaces during school becomes routine and mechanical.

I believe we need to do everything and anything to ensure that students do not take art materials for granted, that they continue to see things with fresh eyes and a sense of playfulness, and that they approach their art tools with a spirit of invention. And, luckily for us, toys are still toys, and when children work with these things not normally associated with school or conventional art classes, they come alive again. Watch what a child does with a new Hot Wheels car: it leaps through the air, skids over the floor, twists and turns to sponta neously invented sound effects. This is true creativity at work, and art materials should be able to generate the same excitement.

Mood and interest improve immediately when I bring in such things as salt and pepper shakers, water pistols, eye droppers, and funnels for students to "draw" with. Even those good old standbys—pencils—are regaining some power these days as unusual designs are being sold all over: pencils are now topped with flamingoes, magician's hats, elephants; some are so large they don't even fit in a standard pencil case.

Materials to Inspire Creativity

Kids in school are used to having art ideas handed to them in the form of lessons, while art supplies are pulled from shipping cartons and distributed from desk to desk. Usually, these supplies are limited to a few specific items chosen on the basis of their efficiency in use and distribution. Teachers are often wary of anything they think will be too messy (e.g., paint) or too playable, which children never want to stop using (e.g., chalk).

Play materials, on the other hand, are what kids dream about, wish for, collect and discover while doing their environmental shopping. They are intended to arouse interest, amazement, involvement, and discovery. And, for that to occur, students themselves should have a say in their selection; if this is not the case, the teacher should take care to choose and present them creatively, setting aside fears that they may be too messy or too difficult to handle, distribute, or transport. Teachers should be importers of special items, selecting things with care, wrapping and packaging with attention, and presenting items to the class with a sense of showmanship. An air of suspense needs to surround materials, not the boredom that ordinarily accompanies the distribution of standard art supplies.

In play classes, then, we first create with play supplies (which can be turned into art supplies) then use art supplies to interpret moods and ideas experienced during play. Children naturally and playfully create not only with bought objects but also with everything they find while gathering environmental treasures. In using play supplies, students approach art supplies more playfully, experimentally, and imaginatively.

A toy car in a child's hands can be driven faster than a crayon and encourages reconsideration of routine "steerings" over art surfaces. Art tools sprout gears to control infinite speed changes and, when fitted with taped on grips, become well-equipped to handle the sharp curves and tight cornering that leave tire marks on test tracks (art surfaces). Moves experienced with matchbox cars enable us to transfer inventiveness and playability to maneuvers with art tools. Each art mark thus represents experiences that feel more real and rehearsed as ideas and moves when danced, skated, or driven beforehand. Play objects and interesting materials speak to their users in many languages, suggesting many possibilities to be played out. The ability to discover and play with objects, to translate from play finds, repeatedly illustrates the nature of the art search.

Teachers must guard against making judgments about the value of specific materials. Children—or art students—just may not share our taste or interests. Certainly, in their independent creative lives—outside of school—children rarely think in terms of art supplies per se. They play with and are interested in everything around them, creating with Band-Aids or paper clips as easily and with as much (perhaps more) pleasure as with clay and markers. Noticing and using what they bring to class underscores the notion that anything can become an exciting source of creative play. Doll playing can be a legitimate part of serious figure exploration; sandbox and block plays are often the road to inventive architecture.

Creative playing with materials begins with the teacher's creative attitude toward them. Use what is already in class—encyclopedias for skyscrapers, rulers for bridges. Envision how an old checkered picnic blanket might look on a gray classroom floor, how a form presented in an unusual basket or locked in a box may be experienced, how an unwrapping ceremony can promote a particular attitude among students. Vague ideas are perfectly acceptable; the more concrete the initial vision, the more limited the possibilities for making art. Students just need to be attracted to play materials, to see their beauty, and to anticipate with pleasure their handling.

If we as art teachers are not a little nervous about this challenge, then perhaps something isn't right. The unpredictable always unnerves. But art, and art making, are supposed to be unpredictable. The teacher too worried about the consequences of using a nontraditional material is not open to the possibility that the kind of enthusiasm it generates will lead to real and energetic creativity. It is as if too much fun means that serious work can't get done. But fun is where seriousness begins, because when we are having fun we are closest to our best selves, where the joyful and creative spirit inspires new visions, new possibilities in the world.

I know a student teacher who used chalk dust as a magic rubbing potion over body tracings. Her students became very involved in the project, but she came under criticism from the teacher, who found the project—with its messiness and the excited classroom activity it engendered—to be just too much trouble. This teacher preferred to maintain a more orderly art class; therefore, she chose to use less exciting materials. But the student teacher confided to me, "I thought the kids loved it and created great art!" She added something very telling, which perhaps gets to the heart of the matter: "I can't work in my studio without an element of mess."

We want to develop artists, and artists must confront the problems and challenges of material: its selection, combination, tools (required and viable), and performance stages (from paper or canvas to almost any other surface available). These are choices that must be made by the individual. Utilizing play materials in the classroom helps students approach art not as a skill or as a technical or physical task but as a challenge that induces inspiration and creative thinking on their part.

Creative Sources for Art and Play Materials

Traditional art materials tell us what art is or has been; play art materials suggest what art can be. In selecting play materials for our students, we must see the children, picture the object's users, and envision the possibilities of play. Many children's things can be used to make children's art, as we expand on what they collect, what they have already discovered, what they have fun with, and perhaps even what they are scared of. The concern manifested in our decisions to collect certain objects invests them with special power, makes them extraordinary. Play materials allow the sharing of something special between special persons: artist to artist, teacher to student.

Sources from Home
It is not a coincidence that our most productive play and art times both occur before we enter school. School art supplies can and should be supplemented by supplies from the richer world of home. Kitchen utensils are a good place to start; we are all graduates of the best "art schools," having once been pots and pans players, block builders, and toy figure arrangers. We may not recall the last

Umbrella City on a Rainy Day

time we were permitted to freely open up cabinets and play with items found there, but surprising uses can be found for a hand mixer, an eggbeater, or a nest of plastic bowls.

Use of Props

"It's for you," the teacher announces as she transfers a call to the red play phone on the student's desk. Students are taking orders from each other for artworks. This is fantasy art play, and it uses a simple prop to explore a conceptual art plan, to involve students in experiencing art-as-idea.

Using plastic sheets as ice to skate on, brown wrapping paper as earth to farm, or white paper tablecloths as operating rooms in which to explore the insides of bodies (through tracing) demands creative interpretation on the part of the student. A plastic garbage bag can become a mountain or a mound of snow, a box of old keys can lead to visions of unusual doors and places that each key may unlock; feathers, scissors, chopsticks, and dust mops can replace traditional drawing tools or paint brushes. Using props may not be the same as clarifying a lesson with a single message, but—unlike standard art materials with established uses—play materials spark a variety of experiences and independent investigations that promote discovery and the possibility for new art.

School art materials lead students too quickly to abstractions before ideas have a chance to be formulated, movements rehearsed, or fantasies explored. Playing with real things—household items, skateboards, sleds, or beach toys—allows students to develop their own interests using objects close to their own experiences. Each play material has suggestive powers and can be used as itself, as an art tool, as a model, or perhaps as a canvas. For example, pickup-sticks can be used as drawing tools (when dipped into media), allowing students to try drawing with many sticks, creating tracks and paths and newly invented finger holds. The sticks can also become batons for musical plays, antennas for make-believe reception of outer space messages, or they can be observed as they are dropped into accidental patterns on the school floor. They can also be balanced in juggling "plays" or patterned stylistically in geometric floor works.

The Artist-Teacher as Source

Inviting students to our homes or offices or bringing our favorite objects in to the classroom can both be worthwhile lessons. Showing future artists how we live, how we shop and find materials, how we display our collections to inspire us in our work is an essential aspect of play teaching. The red play phone referred to earlier in this chapter, for example, is from my own collection. Some have musical ringers; some are takeoffs on phone designs of the 1940s and 1950s; some are actually phone banks.

Whether toy phones or simple paper clips, objects that teachers bring in to class should be selected not just for playability but for beauty as well. What we choose teaches students a powerful lesson about design and culture. Whether objects reflect a historical design or the latest fashion or trend, students should be interested in the range of creativity they imply.

Show-and-Tell

The sharing of finds is an important art room experience for artists of all ages. Not just teachers but students may have objects to share. Students may have favorite objects that they approach with their own play ideas. Sharing these special objects with their classmates gives them a chance to show off their expertise, while the other students can contribute their own best ideas about how to use them.

My Boxes of Play Supplies

My office looks more like a child's room than an official studio. Lining its shelves are boxes whose labels boldly announce their contents:

- balls
- birthday parties 1957–59
- blocks
- buttons

My Office: A Player's Dream Supply Room

- dolls
- juggling supplies
- lunchboxes
- masks
- Matchbox cars
- miniatures
- non-collectible items
- Play Dough
- sticky stuff
- receipts
- robots
- soundmakers
- souvenirs 1960–62
- tents
- toy art supplies
- wizardy equipment

These boxes are filled with the results of years of searching for play materials at local flea markets, neighborhood garage sales, and variety stores, of collecting the toy boxes and wrappers that nobody wants after a birthday party.

Casual browsing in my play boxes can be as pleasurable as the dramatic presentation of a single item, since each box contains clues to special memories. Every object has played many roles; every one has participated in varied adventures.

The items in my boxes are in no way retired or useless—that is their beauty. They live on, ready to take part in adventures with many other people; their shelf life is indefinite. These supplies can never be used up as long as inventive artists and teachers approach them with curiosity and a willingness to present them playfully to receptive students.

My collection is far from complete; I continually add new items to existing boxes and even start new ones, baptizing them in private ceremonies. The longer an item stays in a box, the more important it becomes to me, having withstood the test of time and a variety of players. Periodically, though, I do remove items. Sometimes, I may find something, keep it for a while, and share it later when the time seems right. An object that stays in a box unused for a time can age well and be that much more valuable when it is rediscovered and brought back into the light of day.

Every time an item is returned to its box, having been used in a new way, taken on another identity and use, it is richer for the experience. I try as best I can to keep track of these various histories. Let me share a few of them. Perhaps they will generate ideas for you and, in turn, for your students.

The Buttons Box

I have had a button box for as long as I can remember. As a child, I traded buttons, dressed them with pictures of my soccer heroes, and kept them with me as good luck charms during championship games. Buttons can become jewelry, foreign currency, and alien space ships. They are part of a more general category of miniature play sources and can always stand in as foot soldiers in an army or participants in a masquerade ball. My buttons box contains gold and ivory buttons, shiny and dull ones, large and small buttons. They provide examples of unusual inventions; they are a mark of changing fashion; they show diversity in taste and style. This box also holds fishing sinkers in elegant shapes, colorful golf tees, and bag ties.

The Receipts Box

A container that holds a sea of receipts and other official-looking papers would ordinarily be greeted with dread by most people—but my receipts box offers many play suggestions, including phone messages from make-believe movie stars or creatures, menu pads for taking orders in restaurants, tickets to imaginary concerts, and so on. The day I brought my car home from the garage, I was not happy with the high repair bill, but my pain was mitigated somewhat by the bright-orange, numbered window tag that I was able to add to my receipts box that day. Along with it, I included a soft-paper protective floor mat with unusual oily footprints on it—you never know when something like that will come in handy for a fantasy play! Unusually patterned papers, business forms, carbon backings, perforated cardboard, different kinds of receipt pads—all culled from everyday life—can become extraordinary props for invented play in the art classroom and springboards for any number of ideas.

The Lunchbox Box

Lunchboxes are special. They are children's important private chambers, portable billboards for their favorite films, sports heroes, rock stars, and cartoon shows. They are reminders of their secure home worlds and safe-deposit boxes for their personal mementoes and play objects. They are the last safe place to secrete away favorite images and items usually thought to be trivial distractions. And, of course, they are also repositories for their favorite foods.

I have a lunchbox collection, and, within each lunchbox, I keep treasures that mirror the kinds of things children keep in theirs—Matchbox cars, raisin figures, smelly erasers, Garbage Pail cards. I sometimes imagine that when these lunchboxes are alone together, they secretly trade their contents—and I am never sure when I open one of them what will be inside!

I try to keep my collection current with the latest in lunchbox design. Recently I added a lunchbox camera with a thermos film winder and a small food-storage unit that acts as a changeable lens. Lunchboxes today can double as jukeboxes, trucks, trains, and space stations.

The Play Dough Box

Children like Play Dough because of its many bright colors—including the new Day-Glow soft sets. Unlike clay, which is, of course, considered a professional art material, Play Dough—along with plasticine, Silly Putty, and other soft-sculpture materials—can be played with casually. Students can experiment with these substances—roll them out, squeeze them together, and start all over again. This is much more fun than making a finished art product and taking it home.

In my Play Dough box, I also keep important accessories such as cookie cutters, monster makers, pasta rollers, and other dough-shaping devices. I also keep handy Legos and Bristle Blocks–borrowed from my block box—so that students can make their own presses and use their own hand tools to create playful impressions and stampings in Play Dough manufacturing plants.

In the spirit of soft sculpure, I also keep a variety of bubble makers, bubble gum, slime, spray confetti, and magic sand in this box. Even though chewing gum is not ordinarily permitted in the classroom, sometimes we must allow our children artistic license to break certain rules.

The Mask Box

Oddly enough, I don't keep masks in the mask box—I keep items to transform faces into masks: stickers, Band-Aids, makeup tools, eye patches, shaving creams. Anything that is useful for examining face shapes and watching transformations before a mirror goes into this box.

The Doll Box

Nude models in the elementary school art class may be going too far, but with the twenty-four flexible joints of Ken and Barbie, a whole range of poses is possible. Besides being models, dolls and their wardrobes can be used to mount fashion shows, complete with homes, playgrounds, and performance sets. Dolls can participate in plays and receive art lessons from students (original art by dolls has been exhibited in our classroom with the help of a few stickers to jog the imagination). Some favorites in the collection are Gem and her backup singers (complete with spotlights, instruments, and tapes for classroom concerts), Kewpie dolls, cheerleader paper cutouts, cookie or dried fruit figures, ceremonial dolls, antique ceramic-faced beauties, as well as Pee Wee Herman and Roger Rabbit dolls. This box also contains a videotape by Alexander Calder on famous dolls of early circus stars he created.

The Juggling Supplies Box

Beautiful old monogrammed handkerchiefs with embroidered edges and old designer scarfs from the 1940s and 1950s can be taken from this box to become high-flying paintings or not-so-still-life arrangements to model. Styrofoam cups and multicolored paper plates can be found here as well; sometimes they are juggled on cocktail toothpicks, also found in this box. Balloons in transluscent or metallic colors can be juggled and drawn on at the same time if you use a marking tool to keep them in the air. Juggling supplies are only as limited as the imagination, and this art form has many lessons to teach about form and color patterns.

The Ball Box

If you open this box and see a row of ghoulish faces staring back, don't worry—they're only Madballs, a current fad in face balls. Orange Ping-Pong balls, combined with Velcro stickers—also housed in this box—have been used as building forms. One student used them in a musical composition— a duet with synthesizer and bouncing Ping-Pong balls. A bag of golf balls stained with printing inks have taught a lot about printing and stamping processes. The balls housed in this box are dressed in foils, papers, and fabrics— and some have been or are on their way to becoming three-dimensional canvases.

The Wizard's Secret Box

A sign on this box warns students to open it at their own risk—and the mood is set. Inside? An old black-felt wizard's cone hat. Ziploc bags containing potions (confetti blended with colored sand, glitter, and household spices), an old leather-bound book labeled "Incantations," magic wands, powdered smoke (from model train sets), magic sand, slime, and crystal building sets. Odd-looking (chicken) bones and footprint samples (from cereal box prizes) enable students to imagine all kinds of creatures. Naturally, a little box of plastic spiders is an important tool for our web-drawing artists.

The Block Box

This is probably the heaviest box in my box collection as it houses my own personal wooden block collection. Some of these old wood shapes are peeling and faded, but they are still beautiful with their elegant alphabet carvings. New blocks are well represented too: Lockblocks, Shape Builders, Bristle Blocks, and Legos. Water blocks are the newest addition—forms that stick to each other when wet and can perform gravity-defying feats in water plays and floating parades created by the students. Other items in this box are PVC pipes, brass plumbing connections, magnets, and giant sponges. There is even a package of marshmallows and dog biscuits in soft colors. Additional resources in the block box are copies of *Popular Science* magazine, so that young builders and inventors can explore their own versions—or improvements—of the latest devices.

The Tent Box

This box holds the distinction of being the largest in my collection. There are folding cardboard playhouses, play stores (in panels that easily assemble and disassemble), yard signs, street signs, and real estate signs in this collection. Umbrellas stripped of their fabrics and ready to be re-covered can also be found here for the setting up of a circus or a private studio underneath. There are also smaller-scale bases, houses, and yachts for housing dolls and other figures. Interesting boxes for jewelry or shoes—made from anything from cardboard to tin—are here as well.

The Matchbox Car Box

At first glance, it looks like any other old car graveyard. Piles of automobiles from different years fill the box; some with scratches, others with dents, and a few with drivers still inside. Old replicas, fancy racing cars, and trucks have circled many art room miles. Small fire engines sit alongside tanker trucks. Stamp pads, graphite bins, and rolls of carbon paper are stored beneath all this to record play moves. The cars' twists, turns, skids, and tire marks can be drawn on any number of different highways, speed tracks, and parking lots—with the help of adding-machine tapes or old maps. Just as the American car and highway have populated the dreams of adults, young players find similar freedom in car playing as they execute free-spirited moves and actions that help to inspire their art work. Small cars can turn, corner, and skid—just as art tools do—speeding along to students' sound effects in graceful curves and emotional chases on any surface. Race flags, road signs, stop watches, and miniature orange cones are some of the accessories collected in this box.

The Souvenir Box

This is probably the most personal box, it houses the stuff of dreams, family histories, and travel mementos. Memories are an important source of material for the creation of art. During class reminiscences, we share, create, and envision our mementos. Students are fascinated at seeing their teacher's old art-school class portrait, report card, and autograph book, camp photos, shots of early art works, and souvenir postcards. One tiny toy saved in this box I held in my pocket during my family's escape from Hungary. A miniature souvenir television set bought during my first visit to the Bronx zoo and place mats, menus, and matchbooks from favorite restaurants all trigger personal recollections that I recount to the class. Also in this box are postcards and photos of my uncle's turn-of-the-century luncheonette (complete with advertisements and sugar dispensers), old cereal boxes, a photo of my Aunt Sara's table, baby pictures, and a computer picture from a world's fair. And whenever we take a class trip, we pay serious attention to gift shops for souvenir items that may be candidates for this box for media, canvases, or art forms for our play and art activities.

The Miniatures Box

A famous violinist gave a presentation to a class of children; he began by showing them his first violin. He tried to place his fingers on the strings, but they covered the entire instrument. The children were fascinated by the tiny violin, and all of them wanted to try playing it.

A similar enthusiasm is evident when I hold up any of the tiny items in my box of miniatures—such as a miniature shopping bag that can carry only a single popcorn, the world's smallest pencil and eraser, and my collection of tiny tea sets in plastic and hand-painted porcelain. These items evoke memories of small worlds from Snow White's to Lilliput. They arouse students to imagine the impossible and the fantastic; they think about the possibility of being able to paint so small.

A box containing enlarged views of our world could be equally fascinating. The works of Claes Oldenburg come to mind.

The Soundmakers Box

Children are natural sound-effects makers and will often use both their toys and their mouths to make playful imitations of sounds they know and sounds they invent. In this box, I keep old bicycle horns, bells, rattles in unusual colors, an old toy typewriter, bird callers of various shapes and sizes, pull toys in various states of disrepair, electric hand mixers, and painted tin noisemakers from many a New Year's Eve. An old collapsible music stand and baton lie on top of this pile. Using the variety of items from this box in simple sound experiments we call rehearsals, helps student artists tune up for a drawing or printing session and their own rhythmic exploration of an art surface.

The Robot Box

Among the items in this box are windup units with sparkling chests, remote-controlled smoking, speaking, and shooting models, discarded remote control units from television sets, garage door openers, walkie-talkies, play phones, old toy Transformers, and an old Atari video game with cartridges. Using batteries, voice commands, or the sounds of children, these robots—or their arms and hands—can come to life, move at different speeds, and even make art, if they are equipped with tools. Students come to life as well when they imitate robots and robot movements. As robot technology is continually moving forward, students have available a steady stream of resources with which they can invent art and move freely into new image-making technologies.

The Toy Art Supplies Box

At first opening, students may be surprised that this is called an art supply box. Windup cars, warriors, finger toys, and lipstick need closer inspection before it becomes clear that these are just new forms of crayon to draw with. Plastic ladybugs and other palm-sized creatures with openings on their backs require a second look; then students see that, with pencil inserts, these motorized forms become drawing tools that create different stitches and patterns. Students may utilize the motorized drawing tools or extend their own drawing movements as they add make-believe speeds and patterns to their drawing or erasing. A large representation of the entire Etch-a-Sketch family with its many new magnetic-type descendants such as Magna-Doodle, Magic Sketch, and other plotting devices is for animating diaries of underwater journeys or space adventures. Each art toy suggests may uses.

For example, Swirl Art—a motorized revolving painting disk—has been adapted to become a revolving refrigerator shelf, and spinning lazy Susans become challenging surfaces to paint on. Spiro-Tot, which is a stencil drawing toy series—is represented in the box but so are many architectural and engineering stencils that expand the toy's capabilities

As a child, I loved to stick combs and brushes together in construction plays long before Bristle Blocks were invented. Art toys sold often inspire classroom plays or even remind one of typical kids' inventions that bring about a toy design. I like to hold the toy in the box with many examples of the combs and brushes and other items of related children's play. The art toy aisle is regularly monitored by all our play teachers.

The Non-collectible Items Boxes

Recently, Ivan Chermayeff, the famous American corporate designer who put the red O in Mobil, showed off his private artworks. Displayed were found work gloves clipped to boards with wooden clothespins, discarded wine-cork wrappers rolled into free-form sphinxes and bearded creatures. A tapestry from dozens of airline tickets and a variety of other disparate things that "looked good" were displayed as provocative objects. The collection looked as if

Chermayeff had just assembled it from the fruits of his latest treasure hunt—which were remarkably similar to the contents of most kids' pockets.

Several boxes in my office labeled "non-collectible items" contain things that wouldn't have value in an antique show or that no one would expect anyone, except perhaps a child, to save or even notice. Instead of being affixed to display panels as at the above show, these items remain in boxes waiting to be sorted, and played with, and rediscovered by young artists.

In these boxes are such items as old bicycle and car mirrors—magic places to be looked into. Bubble-gum-machine prizes and discarded puzzle shapes, some still accidentally stuck together, make unusual forms. There are buttons with slogans that have been marked on and graffitied over during searches for new images, celebrities, or sayings. Tiny makeup brushes are unusual brush sets. Band-Aids of all types, smells, and patterns are kid's jewelry. Hangers, pulleys, clothespins of all kinds, hooks, and springs are all available for players ready to come up with imaginative attachments or idea collections.

Overall, this box smells good because it has absorbed the fragrances of smelly stickers, scented erasers, and perfume samples. Smelly artworks encourage the discovery of monsters, for example, tracked down through a variety of clues, including footprints from our collection (cutouts from cereal boxes). With all the new colors of Slinkys and sporting-events tickets, the big problem here is—should another box be started?

Presentation of Materials

Rolling a collection of balls into the art room always means losing a few along the way as they fall through the sides of my shopping cart. But the attrition is a small price to pay for the instant attention sparked by my unconventional entrance. Play objects should be introduced with a great deal of showmanship. Place an obviously heavy object in a sack and roll it in on a toy cart; carry in something mysterious wrapped in a wet beach towel or securely padlocked inside a sturdy box. Start on the floor discovering a carefully planned "accident" and then go to the table to unwrap the surprise. Dress items for view and sequence them for gradual introduction throughout the class, not just at the beginning. A fanfare should accompany the arrival of each object—something could arrive claiming magical qualities or be presented through an unusual tale or a playful skit. Once revealed, objects can gain new interest from the way we creatively transport them from one place to another. An aura of excitement should surround play objects right from the start and throughout the session. Our delight in them will make them all the more appealing to the student-artists whose creativity they are intended to awaken.

Movements and Fantasies

Movement

◆

When I was a youngster, I remember looking intently at Duchamp's *Nude Descending a Staircase* during our first school museum trip. I knew that this landmark futurist work was supposed to communicate movement, but it didn't say anything to me. The action paintings in the next room were equally disappointing; all failed to reveal action to me—or I failed to see it. I continued to be unmoved by action in art until I began teaching, when I first studied the chase scenes in children's drawings. The trees moved—the whole earth crackled—as characters yelled and raced across the surface of the paper. It seemed to me then that only children knew how to put themselves and their real actions on paper—and that they did so intuitively. Movement in adult art, by contrast, is diagrammed and theoretical, active only when compared to other, even more frozen, adult art. But children are able to jump into their pictures and really describe dancing and other such activities, without a formula. Kids are natural animators because they live in animated states.

The Freezing of Movement in Children's Classroom Art

Action art may begin with children's earliest works, but it tends to go underground as kids grow older: Their cartoons and caricatures often aren't appreciated by the purveyors of so-called appropriate art. Their humorous works are likely to end up under their desks, inside their notebooks, or in secret notes.

In most art classes, students are quickly seated, and, thereafter, few movements are allowed. The attitudes of teachers in the conventional art classroom are very telling:

> Kids have a special energy which needs to be controlled. They come to class jumping, moving, and wanting to touch everything. That's okay in gym class and I often advise parents to enroll their kids in some sport. They dance through the aisles, and I think: maybe a dance class would be better for them. But in the art class, I wish they could just sit still!

The teacher speaking here is involved in a daily struggle to contain and slow down that which is most natural: the playful and experimental movements of children. Yet when we try to hold children back, we are failing to recognize that their very movements carry creative possibilities that can contribute profoundly to their art making. Children move through their environments with arms outstretched, searching and drawing with their bodies long before they get to a piece of paper.

Whereas some teachers are nervous about movement in the classroom, others are equally nervous about sound—or what they perhaps call noise. For example: "Oh, those drumming sounds of kids beating on the table! They can cause the dead to move! They are driving me crazy in class!" But sound effects made by busy hands and busy mouths are a natural accompaniment to students' movements and an effective counterpoint to their creative restlessness. Children use movement and sound together to inspire their particular artistic inventiveness on the page and elsewhere.

Teachers often complain that "kids have no patience to sit still." They blame video games ("They stare at them for hours at a time!") or cartoons ("They watch them all the time; it makes them crazy!") or television in general ("Kids watch too much television and the programs are a waste of time").

But dismissing the interests and play inspirations of today's generation of children is the same as ignoring their most immediate, fundamental, and direct sources of art. In the name of higher art standards and ideals, teachers too often choose to discount the new generation of players who have grown up before fast-moving screens and who are able to control images with joy sticks at lightning speed.

If you stay long enough in art school, you begin to take yourself—and art—too seriously. It is hard to compete with Picasso, and worrying about contributing to the existing art world can be paralyzing. Art cannot be fun if we carry the burdens and theories of the art world on our shoulders—and transfer them to our students. The school art classroom should not be an art academy, drained of the fun that best exemplifies children's art. Kids bring active bodies, vivid fantasies, and dreams of moving images to class. It is funny kids, playful kids, who create the unique art we call children's art.

The Art Classroom in Motion

At its best, children's art expresses the fast heartbeats and inner rhythms that power their playful moves and, by extension, their art. We should try to harness these movements, not struggle to stamp them out. Instead of teaching movement theories, we should keep moving in our classes—a far better way to learn about making moving images. We should search through children's repertoires of favorite movements for characters and adventures that will convincingly help us descend stairs. Children's play activities should come into the art room, as movement over surfaces—whether that of bodies moving across the floor or paint across paper—is explored.

In play classes, kids move all the time. We plan artworks to be brief and we intertwine them with playing throughout the class period. Rather than considering the movement of an object a disturbance—as is often the case in

Rock-n-Roll Plays

a conventional classroom—we teach objects to move, we wind them up, bounce them, and explore them as they roll across the floor. Rather than encouraging silence—as is done in most conventional classrooms—we encourage sounds and moving accompaniments; sometimes we play music—not to soothe, but to excite. Acting, dancing, moving in the aisles are means of gathering ideas and preparing for art.

We play-art teachers use classrooms as rehearsal studios and dance floors. We cast aside worries about seating arrangements and learn to enjoy our students' movement and to move with them playfully in games, dances, and patterns. We learn to think of art as animation as we move lines, tools, and our bodies across the room or over a piece of paper. We adapt our own live animation from our movements in space to the two dimensions of a drawing paper. Today's technology has allowed children to switch into higher play modes, action gears, and sophisticated sound effects—all of which inevitably affect their play interests, movements, and, by extension, their art. We should learn from all aspects of the new animation and action-toy world. Moving children are not annoying or distracting from classroom activity. We are not here to control students' active moves but to applaud their performances and organize them into art follow-ups.

The Moving Body as Art Tool

Calisthenics

During my school years in Vienna, we began each session with simple calisthenics. Unfortunately, this was followed by the copying of still images onto graph paper. But today's Nike-wearing art teacher can use the body as a teaching tool: snapping, tapping, taking the lead in a parade. Movement not only warms up sleepy bodies, it also generates ideas and impressions, all of which continue onto art surfaces. Moving bodies easily translate into moving attitudes and moving images as students become freer and more willing to make rapid crossings and changes in their art.

Changes of speed, creative rushing or slowing down, winding up and activating each other can catalyze an art lesson. Activities like jumping rope are useful, too: students can study the patterns of the rope, the shapes drawn in the air, and the new movements invented through the process. Smaller strings attached to art tools can capture these sights and rhythms so that the vision and feeling of a particular movement can persist and inspire beyond the act itself.

Dance

I recently filmed a video of a five-year-old child in a pink tutu in the act of inventive dancing while making art. To hot Latin beats, she danced in the backyard while tracing stickers on an empty box. She then colored the box, never missing a beat and stopping only occasionally to dance with the box as her partner.

Choreographers have long used the movements, inventions, and fantasies of children in dance compositions. Why shouldn't art teachers take advantage of the talent of the dancers in their classrooms and incorporate their movements into the art lessons? Choreographed entrances and deliberately invented ways to cross a room can move onto art surfaces. Fantasies of moving bodies can extend to art tools, and vice versa.

Observe the creativity that is on display at any school dance. Kids show off their style, display their moves, and invent new steps. Unlike the generation before them, which went to school to learn the proper steps, today's young people use the floor as a canvas, painting it with original dance moves. An art room should have the spirit of a school dance, where joyous inventors gather to create new steps.

Groups can be organized to move in directed ways: in lines shoulder to shoulder, linked as a train, in varied rows, and hand-holding formations. Factory play lines can be organized in teams or crews to move in joined rhythm according to a script or specific challenge. Make-believe rides, crossings, or adventures can promote individual explorations within group activities. Magic carpet rides, soaring landings and take-offs, windup people and machinery allow play to move through space with diverse speeds and movement patterns. Alternations in settings or spaces invite new responses. Spaces can be divided by means of partitions, lighting, and furniture. Paths and corridors for specific movements can be designated with tapes, arrows, or spaces connected and separated, opened or enclosed, with canvas, fabric, or other materials.

Imitation and Fantasy

Children have unusual abilities to visualize movements and throw themselves into movement roles, remembering and imitating moves they have seen at other times and places. Watch them work to perfect moves in a city basketball court, originating ball-handling steps even professionals would admire, or unleash their comic selves as they imitate the wobbling of an old windup toy or rehearse the funny walk of a cartoon character. Dancing brooms and talking art tools continue onto art surfaces as a playful attitude becomes part of students' artistic personalities.

Moving stirs the body and mind to explore, to find the new. Encourage movements that are slow, quick, loud, silent, heavy, soft, sad, or joyful. Test out different surfaces: walking on screens, shingles, sponges, soft paper towels. Imitations of animals help us focus in our movement plays. Creep like a mouse; crawl like a caterpillar; hop like a cricket; gallop like a pony. In drawing our twists and turns, jumps and hops, we become more confident in our movements over art surfaces, and we benefit from the elegant variety of line movements, patterns, and directions stemming from our initial movement rehearsals.

Acting out simple stories, students can become anything and everything—from robots to helicopter pilots. Pantomime allows them to try out different parts—they can flex different muscles, use different body parts in each performance. Any machine is worth studying, any act of nature. Both a waterfall and a lawn mower suggest new moves or drawings. Imagine being a tree. Now you're being swayed by the wind. Then, it's raining, and you're losing all your leaves, while trying hard to turn toward the sun. Feeling forced to change elicits playful moves, and all this easily and naturally filters into art.

Move away from the school desk to a make-believe pool or sandpile. Desks can become tunnels to crawl through; chairs can act as runways to take off from; students can leap over things like cracks in the linoleum or strategically placed books. Umbrellas can be parachutes; suspended blankets can be tents.

Sounds

Sounds inspire movement and improve the rhythms and timing of art. Sounds suggest pauses, moods, and even speeds and directions for moving our hands while creating a work. But silence is the necessary pause to which sounds are contrasted. And so we need to experience silence in the classroom and build sounds from it.

A variety of sounds help us study how sounds relate to space. For example, through whispering, singing, noisy chattering, and other sounds, a collection of party noisemakers invites live participation from the curious. After musical tryouts and loud jamming sessions, students explore the difference between loud and quiet drawings. Making up words, trying out tongue twisters, imitating foreign sounds, and making up funny voices help students feel the texture of sounds. Scat singing, imitations of environmental noises, and synthesizer plays encourage inner sounds and movement improvisations.

The body itself is a sound-making instrument that all students use, and, as they clap, snap, whistle, or drum, they explore the uses of teeth, mouth, nose, hands, and feet. Students who think of themselves as composers approach drawings with great freedom; crossing an art surface becomes a planned and felt musical affair. A drawing, in fact, can be conducted, rehearsed, and even choreographed for its sounds.

Our composing talents are multifaceted. As musical composers of soundscapes before landscapes and sound portraits before art portraits, we play with toys, appliances, and even noisemakers, collecting environmental clues and sound tracks for new artworks. We record the sounds of a busy class at work or the pleasant singing of a spring bird. Playground sounds or the roar of subway trains travel through class speakers and then pass through our minds into our art. We search for the sound in everything, noting the sounds necessary to draw a dot or line or to produce the brush strokes in a painting. We compose sound pictures and create visual pictures from listening to sounds. Class slide shows or fashion shows or shadow performances all are integrated with music; we admire artworks through sound tributes; we experience a great master's art by being inspired to make music to it. We set up plays to experience our own rhythms or to discover new rhythms for our movements and, consequently, the marks we make on an art surface.

Children's moves and visualizations are very close to the sounds they make. And just as sounds bring children's play alive, making it fun and imaginative so they can lend similar vitality to children's art. Moving to a single sound, a pattern of repeated sounds, or to their own music can bring art to life.

Hands, Fingers, Arms, Feet

Fingers can be dressed in makeup, nail polish, and stickers as they kick up a storm. Hands can playfully control make-believe joysticks in a fast-moving arcade game. Hands can dance as shadow performers or slow-motion sculpture. They can tickle, snap, point, rub, or tap. They can be used inventively to clap as if discovering new ways of performing this familiar sound effect. They can balance objects or tools or grip them in inventive patterns. Arms can playfully stretch, pound, tug, sweep, pull, shake, scrub, or swing.

Playful art tools can extend playful hands and fingers in scratching and rubbing over surfaces. They can be clapped together or moved in sync with inventive arm dances. Pauses and rhythms can be clapped out as well as designed over art surfaces. Art surfaces can be sparred with, stretched, or engaged in a tug-of-war as lines are pulled across them.

Kicking (like the Rockettes or in karate moves), tapping toes, clapping heels, standing on tiptoes, or skipping on one foot are some of the many leg and foot movements awaiting playful rehearsals. Art tools between toes, stamping with shoes on, tiptoeing over surfaces or skating with art tools tied to one's feet are some of the inventions students have arrived at while considering the possibilities of extending movement into art.

Cartoons and Animation

Children are natural animators. They bring dolls, teddy bears, G.I. Joes, and California Raisins to life. They talk through them, make them dance, involve them in adventures. Kids prefer toys that move—that can be posed, wound up, remote-controlled, and acted with. Today's toys can be programmed, transformed, walked—and many can talk back. Figures have more joints, dolls have larger vocabularies, and pull toys perform more acrobatics than ever before. Kids' fantasies are embodied in television characters: for example, Pee Wee Herman videos can be extended with actions in his playhouse using his many props and figures. Most films for children have plenty of souvenirs and related toys so that kids can extend them into play at home or in art class.

In the art classroom, we may audition new cartoon stars as we place tiny eyes on pencils, a tea kettle, a fire extinguisher, a mixer, or other objects in the room. We animate ourselves as we put on plastic noses and act out new characters for art adventures. A lesson can be presented without talk using sounds, signs, and movement. A drawing might use a laugh track or a special effect as its movement inspiration. We know cartoons can move and talk, but can they draw? Who can teach them? Can a cartoon sit on your pencil? Who is in control now? Each antic of a cartoon or performance of a star can be imitated in art action as we teach our cartoon bodies a thing or two. As cartoons, we can move anywhere, chase anything, climb over any art room surface, or jump on any art room material; lines, like cartoons, can travel. Each mark can stretch, skid, or take off in any direction. A drawing tool can have stilts, be bounced by a pogo stick, or zapped by a laser gun in preparation for a drawing. We can cheer, clap, twirl our pencils, propel tools at different speeds, or launch them from different heights as we visualize a variety of impressions.

Ideas for Movement Plays

Toys as Inspiration

Many toys—old and new—can be the inspiration for in-class movement plays. Battery-operated cars, windup horses, and robots are examples. Teachers and

Inventing and Recording New Games

students alike should be on the alert for garage sales as well as keeping tabs on the latest inventory of local toy stores. Never throw away old toys before considering the movement fantasies they might evoke for imaginative students. Below are some examples of toy-inspired plays we've seen work magic on sleepy students.

- ◆ You spot Lucy and Desi driving in a blue Rolls bumper car. While Desi turns the steering wheel, Lucy occasionally turns herself to snap a picture. The battery-operated car with working headlights moves in random patterns, bumping into objects as it swerves in new directions. Students get into their own cars—a variety of vehicles, some with only steering wheels (garbage can covers), others with only a body (cardboard boxes held around the students' necks by string), still others sporty convertibles (chairs lying on their backs)—and try to avoid colliding with Lucy's car. Over paper highways, tiny cars lead the way to drawing drives led by Lucy and Desi in their old, tiny toy careening in crazy patterns.

◆ Hi-o Silver! But the tiny horse high on its hind legs is bright green, not silver white. As the windup horse rears up and down, its riding acrobat rotates colorful rings and swirls larger hoops attached to its sombrero. We mount our own horses in pursuit as we saddle our chairs. Students find it fun to try to stay seated while juggling cups and twirling lariats. We try to keep our horses steady as we attempt to outmaneuver the skillful little toy at center stage.

◆ While walking, smoking, and spinning, one fellow talks to another with a movie monitor on his chest. Who is controlling what is hard to tell at this convention of robots. Toy robots of all kinds show off their talents as students press buttons, wind up keys, or utter voice commands. Soon, other robots join the act; some wobble like penguins as students learn the fine points of remote-controlling one another. Fun and laughter abound as we rehearse movements and windup actions.

◆ Zippo the monkey, a fifty-year-old Louis Marx toy with great exaggerated moves, climbs a rope then slowly glides down into the hands of its trainer. With strings (make-believe ropes) hanging from classroom ceilings, student acrobats demonstrate their own slow-motion climbing techniques. Many new and old acrobatic toys chin and balance or move across parallel bars, suggesting art moves and pantomime inspirations. Tiny toy creations in performance allow bodies and pencil gymnastics to alter art moves.

◆ High above, leaping through the air from a platform slope, is one of my favorites, a tiny somersaulting ski jumper who flies through the air yet always manages to land on two skis. This fabulous spring-loaded toy has prompted many Olympics plays where students jump over paper inclines with art tools in hand. Winter plays—drawing with gloved hands, arms outstretched, knees bent, and minds sailing free—are also inspired by our little ski jumper.

◆ Step right up, ladies and gents, to experience the world's greatest roller coaster (or ferris wheel, or carousel)! Each spinning at its own rate and rattling with a clang, these colorfully imprinted beer-can toys were made during the war years when metal was in short supply. As painted faces and creatures speed by, we imagine all types of circling and fast-action playing. To experience these moves, we hold hands in a circle around the carnival, looping up and down and reversing until we get dizzy. Driving a drawing tool around a track or mounting one to a carousel (make-believe, of course) lead to all kinds of circular crossings and inventive spiraling.

◆ In our school desks, many work horses wait, ready to build roads, construct buildings, and plow fields. Cement mixers, bulldozers, cranes, and tractors with their full array of implements await their work orders. Students receive job slips and move out onto highways (paper rolls) or over the brown earth (brown wrapping paper). Some toy trucks have drawing-tool attachments that help workers in construction helmets leave the marks and traces of a job well done. Toy moves can be traced or followed by drawing moves or even occur over carbon paper laid over drawing surfaces. We can plan some moves by laying out plastic tape or metal train tracks to cross.

* On the gray waters of our classroom floor, you can find all kinds of crafts sailing by. A sound blast comes from a Mississippi steamer spouting smoke pellets as it goes by. Above it in the classroom sky, there is a cable car, small occupants waving. In imagining what each ride would feel like, we can become part of any toy adventure. Holding straps attached to a clothesline on pulleys, we feel our ride. We sit on a raft or inner tubes to follow the boats. As we count down and watch the launching of a battery-operated space ship, we can also launch our drawing tools and bodies to sympathetic actions.

* Watch out for ducks! On a revolving boat inside a colorful action stage rotates a row of ducks inside a target game. The shooting gallery has many moving parts to hit and score, bend and ping, spin or bounce off the target line. We form our own duck line, holding hands, bobbing and weaving, as another line of hunters fires make-believe shots. Later, kids savor each funny sequence as it pops out of their art tools.

Videotape Players

California Raisins on tour are now appearing in the classroom courtesy of videotape recordings. Favorite plays with teddy bears, or dolls at a tea party, or a fashion show for Barbie can all be recorded and brought to the screen. Cutout paper-doll fashion shows will never be the same after they become part of a television talk show.

TV cameras in play classes risk having nervous breakdowns, since the audience keeps turning into the performers. Playing becomes more exciting before a camera. Because it captures moving images, television forces students to think in terms of active playing and image making. Still art becomes performance as we dance with pencils or twist and turn to music while wearing our canvases. We teach art tools to move and observe art moves with cameras thirsty for action.

Today, we're able to screen the finest cartoons in class because they're available as inexpensive movie rentals. Using the control buttons on the VCR to reverse, fast-forward, pause, rewind, and slow down action makes for all kinds of viewing fun and art ideas. Feeling in control of the moving images on a screen promotes a more playful and active attitude toward art images on any art surface.

Sketching from a monitor, students can participate in actions on the screen by following the movements of cartoons, gymnasts, or dancers. Pointing and drawing in the air or tracing and diagramming action, we can follow the changing faces, gestures, and expressions on the screen. Using the monitor as a light box, we can study the lines and details of movements, editing, overlapping, and assembling our own sequences. Drawing from the monitor on television pads like those used by professionals or on screen-shaped pages of our own design, we can be camera persons, editors, or directors. (For continuous recordings, we prefer paper rolls pulled from dispensers we call art cassettes.) Sometimes we wrap a monitor and draw on the paper, letting the sounds lead our tools.

When cartoons jump from the screen—sometimes we dare them to escape—we follow their mischief in person over paper rolls and runways taped to the monitor screen. We extend wires from the television antennae to our drawing papers in attempts to catch characters from the air waves before they slip into the set.

We tune into the sounds of drawing acts and also make purposeful sounds to consider sound tracks for artworks. We explore all sources that suggest interesting art moves and try out different tools, sounds, timing and muscles in planning and directing movement ideas. We act out and fantasize movements through toys, people and objects. We play with movement words as we outrace a train, a speeding bullet, drawing at laser speeds. We tune into moves, rehearse movements, and move sympathetically to the moves we observe and experience.

Musical Instruments

With hands in position, shoulders straight, we move pencils up and down to the rhythms of a violin piece. Gliding over surfaces, stroking, and crossing with our bows, we re-experience familiar art tools. We test surfaces by drumming on them, identifying new ones by the way they sound. With bottle caps attached to our shoes, we perform our drawings and later tap them out with crayons. The varied speeds and sounds of three blenders become a symphony, the score of which is blended, twirled, and spun into artworks. We explore the musical potential of blow dryers through duets with synthesizers. Blowing through plastic drain pipes, conducting a radio with art tools, or recording the movements of a whistling top as it moves across an art surface inspires our playing. Students accompany their rock-and-roll art with bells, whistles, and noise-makers. With musical pull toys, we drag melodious lines and shapes across paper. Using tape, bicycle handles, gloves, and vacuum cleaner tubes, we lengthen strokes and extend our reach in imitation of bows, drumsticks, or conductor's batons. With electric instruments as models, we electrify art tools, motorize movements, amplify markings, and plug into new imaginative actions.

We are always looking for new instruments to play, training all objects to make sounds and musical patterns.

Art Class Aerobics

Bend and stretch and reach for the stars! Following video exercise tapes, we get down on the floor to move and make art. Our mats on the floor are rolls of paper, and our back stretching and knee bending lead to the discovery of new art lines. We crawl like newborns, discovering our toes and fingertips for the first time. We hold hands to synchronize art moves. Moving across the patterned art room floor, we become chess pieces, hurdlers, or dancers on tiptoes. Other lines move like dragons in a Chinese New Year parade, twirling art tools in fierce locomotion. We run in circles around paper tracks and climb from the bottom to the top of each page. Still lifes move as we balance, juggle, hide, or stack objects in space. Tools move as they are motorized, remote-controlled, or used with extension handles. Canvases move as we walk over them, program them to rotate, or wear them.

Just as movement can inspire art, art marks can inspire movement, dances of pencils, brushes, and bodies. We can move to the works of well-known artists or bring to life our own art fantasies. Art tools can be asked to dance; if they don't know how, we can teach them. We can perform with lines, pulling, tugging, pushing them. We can tangle bodies and lines in play or on paper, creating knots a boy scout has yet to dream of. Lifting weights, we recall the weights of art tools and the loads we carry over art surfaces. In space aerobics, students test the limits of weightlessness as the new state of art.

Art Teams

It is springtime, and everyone is excited about playing outside. How does a batting stance relate to a pencil stance? Art room teams can compete in a variety of sports by adjusting tools and actions for different arenas, rinks, or ski slopes—the new names for our art papers. Controlling fast-paced sports video games, children warm up for action on the art surface.

During special events, we talk and think in terms of movements. Art marks are really hit marks on a backboard as we dribble our tools and bounce on art surfaces. Slope lines are marked by skiers who have dipped poles—pencils and other equipment—in paints, graphite, or chalk dust. Events may start on table-tops—a recent soccer game took place on a paper tablecloth where players moved and recorded their moves. Paper rolls stretched across the classroom for grand prix racing soon show traces of high-speed competition—marks and oil slicks fill the track. With moving hands and closed eyes, we follow the play-by-play reports of various events.

Counting—out loud or to oneself—is a way of signaling and pacing children's play or sports events. Experiment with different speeds, from the comfortable to the unusual or extreme. Use audible timers, hour glasses, or talking clocks to track events. For high-speed plays such as races and chases, use a stop watch and fun items such as a starting flag or a starting gun (a cap pistol). Time challenges make children aware of the visual qualities associated with movements at various speeds. Watching video clips of cycling and track events, they can learn to move in tune to new and expanding movement ideas.

Art players need more room than traditional art makers. Playing before the art requires space and while a small rectangle may be okay for traditional art, those works born in play require open spaces if the play is to continue in the art. An 8″ × 10″ rectangle sheet is too static a confined cell for most sports and plays as we turn to rolls, scrolls, screens and multiple pages for the runways of our gestures. Players naturally innovate with stages to move on as the actions of kids' art breaks into new art invention.

Voice-sampling Synthesizers

"How Much is that Doggie in the Window?" no longer requires backup by live canines. Anything from a lion's roar to the whistle of a passing train or the sound of an entire marching band can be reproduced by low-priced synthesizers in the art class. Students' voices and sound effects can be recorded, scrambled, and replayed with other sounds in arrangements impossible before.

Synthesizer plays help students to think of art making as composing. As we snap and clap and reach into the synthesizer memory bank for different whistles, we recognize the possibilities of rhythm in art. Disney brought the magic of sound to animation, thereby changing the industry; teachers now can add sound tracks to student play and art to revolutionize the art room. The electronic beeps, gurgles, and cheers of video games can be reproduced and used to keep action moving in any art work. Features such as built-in metronomes and drum pads allow students to study the beats of music and art. New keyboards can be stepped on and danced over leaving students' hands free to draw. In addition to synthesizers, many other electronic and musical toys provide audible and visual signals by which to conduct art works. Games like Simon use light signals and buzzing clues that suggest complex rhythm patterns for students to apply in their art inventions. One electronic instrument can replace all the many noisemakers I used to use in play classes to suggest drawing beats, line harmonies, and character actions.

Sound effects help make plays believable. Consider one teacher's experiment in a play class where students were building castles and blocks. First, she announced, "Time for an earthquake," and asked students to draw pictures of themselves amid the rubble. Then, using a synthesizer and sound effects, she stages a minicataclysm, encouraging the class to react to the devastation. The children—and their blocks—flew around the room, caught in the shockwaves or trying to avoid the raging destruction. Some landed in corners; others were thrown to the higher ground of tabletops and chairs or sought cover under desks. The differences in the two sets of drawings were remarkable. In the first set, students simply made pictures of themselves sitting next to fallen blocks.

The second set of pictures showed scenes of wild—and wildly varied—mayhem, as the refugees vividly re-created their own particular experiences of the catastrophe.

Animation

Recently, our six-year-old excitedly announced an impending birth in her school class. She then explained that an egg had been placed in the room to hatch and that the children had to wait for twenty-seven days to see what was inside. Over the following weeks, she eagerly counted down the days, wondering when the egg would break and whether something would fly out or roll out huffing. In honor of my daughter's mystery egg, many variously colored Play Dough eggs now sit in individual boxes on the tables in my classroom. The art class imagines what is inside each egg, then, just as Michelangelo freed his images from marble, we break into our egg forms to discover new action characters. We also give birth to new toons by simply drawing two circles in the air and then on paper, discovering, as Disney did, the magical images that can evolve from such simple origins. We envision new forms taking shape in a drop of paint from a giant basting tube or small eyedropper, picturing how they will come to life through movement. Each newborn character's traits, moves, and personality, as well as what we can teach him or her, becomes part of our discussion.

In search of moves, we study a caterpillar under a magnifying glass or follow videotaped bugs as they crawl across the screen. Through playful imitations, we become elephants or dance like seals. Our goal is to play with and animate everything in the art class. Staplers' mouths open wide as they belt out the latest hits. Tractor chains creep to a synthesizer accompaniment. Apples talk to us as we sculpt them with our teeth. As we animate objects, we also tickle lines, sway with shapes, and snap to rhythmic patterns, similarly animating each element in an artwork.

Conclusion

Art rooms of action recognize that kids are active learners, impatient viewers, and fast-paced players. Instead of designing spectator events, I suggest we initiate experiences where participation in movement is required. Instead of trying to teach patience, utilize the creative *im*patience of young artists. Each class should start with an action, not a speech.

While adult art may describe or suggest movement or imply movement theories, it usually appears contrived when compared with the pure movement expressed in a child's portrait or—frequently—single line. Funny, curious, experimental, or searching movements are expressed directly and preserved in children's drawings and artworks. In such drawings—made through playful movements, inspired by play itself—the moving force of life receives its most beautiful expression.

The Star of Our Show

FIVE

Performance

 • ◆ •

Those of us with children are accustomed to nonstop show-and-tell; their displays celebrate the most unlikely objects, which themselves demonstrate the unlikely ability to walk and talk. We have seen that our children will talk to, dance with, or wear just about anything.

Send a child to the refrigerator, and on the way back to the table the container becomes the Milk Monster. Ask a pair of siblings to bring an extra chair to the dinner table, and the older child carries in the younger child rocking and balancing on the chair in imitation of Chinese acrobats. Ask a child to unwind a hose and watch it become a snake, slithering and hissing at unsuspecting parents. Inspired by commercials and television shows like "Pee Wee's Playhouse," children transform household appliances and home furnishings into props for their performances. Tables are for dwelling under; chairs are for piloting or racing.

Children's play in the home has helped us recognize that creativity in art and play performances are intertwined. Dressing up, staging shows before a mirror, improvising rock concerts, and imitating others are creative performances that relate to, and can be extended to, art.

The Devaluation of Children's Performance Art in School

Too often, teachers view children's performances in school as childish or inappropriate or, at best, as unimportant and unworthy of encouragement. In fact, schools try to slow down or outlaw the acting and improvising that children naturally bring with them wherever they go. Classrooms—quiet, controlled, motionless—are unfriendly places, where children are likely to withdraw their most creative selves of their own accord, even when they aren't told to do so by impatient teachers, wanting to get on with the lesson.

Such an atmosphere is unfortunate in the regular academic classroom; it is no less than inexcusable in the art classroom. We say we want to uncover children's "talent," but their talent is too often confused with their ability to follow adult art instruction. Children are asked to become audiences instead of participants in their artistic lives; in a typical art classroom, their originality is squashed as their performances are put on hold. But it is those performances that are needed to generate ideas for their art. Art teaching becomes a monologue instead of a deliberate invitation to create a stage or search out playful objects that will promote improvisation or stir the imaginations.

Given this training, it is no wonder that the natural performance talents of young children quickly disappear. Children who once enjoyed dressing up, improvising shows, and playing imaginatively with dolls dispense with such activity altogether. In fact, almost all creativity seems to disappear as children learn early that it is safer not to be different. Those who remain natural performers frequently are either cited for acting out or regarded as being overactive.

The Revaluation of Children's Performance Art in School

In our art classes, we aim to change all that. We see performance as a challenge to action, a wake-up call, an invitation to get involved and to participate. We want our students to feel free to play with anything and everything. Performance lets them rehearse their art before they commit it to paper (or whatever). It loosens up both bodies and minds and helps students become aware of how they move over every life stage, whether the surface is real or imagined. From dressing up, dancing, doing imitations, making mouth sounds and gestures, and so on, it is a small but natural leap to playful performance in artworks. Kids learn to leap, spin, and express themselves in a variety of ways with their art tools. Drawing while in the role of a clown or a robot leads to different pressures, speeds, and turns in both two- and three-dimensional space. Even older children will be less shy, less reluctant to perform, when given opportunities to lose themselves in other roles. Well-chosen costumes and props can provide safe havens that relieve the pressures of self-consciousness and encourage free movement.

Older children tend to approach play in thematically traditional ways, namely, through sports, dancing, magic, juggling, clowning, and the like. Don't confuse reluctant play starts with unwillingness. Break down barriers just as you'd break the ice at a school party: personally extend an invitation to the first dance. The rest will come naturally.

Students who associate art with only a narrow set of tools, tasks, and images have more difficulty in play classes. But performing in life relates directly to performance on paper, as lines of one sort are pulled in a tug-of-war, jumped through during jump rope, or manipulated in string games like cat's cradle before lines of another sort appear in a drawing. There *is* a connection.

Through performances in the art class, we return to the notion of *feeling* art, of exploring ideas through our bodies and our actions. We become the artwork before it leaves our bodies as images on paper.

In the conventional art classroom, the words "Don't touch," "Don't move," and "Don't play" result in an art that is unfelt, unexplored, and neither funny nor moving. When students are, instead, invited to break away

Lunch-Box Performances

from the limitations imposed by standard seating and standard school they find a new freedom—and usually a previously unrecognized ability to be creative.

The Art Teacher as Performer

Although art teachers cannot regularly paint or sculpt in front of their classes, they can playfully perform their art-teaching tasks each day. Instead of presenting their subjects in a businesslike manner, they can choose to reveal themselves through their playful actions, private collections, and personal stories, sharing their excitement with those around them. An art teacher's ability to demonstrate his or her own playfulness in the classroom draws out the creativity of other players. As the chief dreamer in the class, he or she must inspire others to seek beyond the obvious.

Teaching as a Creative Act

What do you do in class? I play; I pretend; I make art. I also show, display, package; I take fantasy trips, make up stories, try on things, play house, and design visual experiments. I frequently hide things, prepare unusual settings, create exciting entrances, and rearrange the room.

Dr. Szekely Caught in a Play Act

Art teaching as a creative performance requires the teacher to be an active, playful designer of the environment and of all the objects and performers in it. I try to think up performances for myself that will interest and involve others. These fun-filled, playful performances both demonstrate the creative act and allow students to see someone in the act of being playful and creative.

In my role as performer, I can become anyone or anything and take imaginary trips anywhere at anytime. For example, on a colorful piece of carpet, I may take the class on a magic carpet ride. Using a remote-controlled device, I move the arms and determine the actions of class members. I try out a space capsule made of chairs arranged on the floor. I always have a pocketful of fine rocks, imaginary treasures, or unusual keys to secret places. I blow bubbles, build dreams with magic sand or slime, and play in the dark with Day-Glo strings and blocks. I am willing to try on anything—from a new nose to a pair of 3-D glasses or an unusual crown.

Art is visual, and an art lesson should be an exciting visual performance. Think of the art room as a canvas for your actions as a teacher, as a stage for your art-teaching performance. Art is most influentially taught through you.

Getting out the Message: Playing Is Permitted

Being a player in school requires courage from both teachers and students. Though kids may love to make faces, create sound effects, or perform dances, they are not used to being allowed to bring these behaviors into the classroom. For their part, teachers are not supposed to encourage children to have a good time in school. For them, play may feel risky because it is not considered "adult" or "professional"; certainly, the actions I am recommending will do little to maintain the stern front presented by a typical "serious" teacher.

Most schools tend to enforce sameness and conformity, but a teacher's imaginative performances can break down the barriers. Imagine a teacher coming to a class wearing bright red shoes. Arms outspread, he steps on a chair and leaps to another. As the pilot of a low-flying plane—with a sputtering motor, perhaps—the teacher folds and tears colored shapes of paper—sculptures he is depositing over the terrain. Broadcasting news of each successful drop over the plane's intercom, the pilot requests special assistance from the class to complete his mission of sculpting from the air.

This teacher is demonstrating not only the lesson's theme but also that playing is fun—and permissible. His performance inspires and licenses creative playing in others. Play is simply live art making.

Art Teacher as Clown

Play-art teachers hide things, try on unusual items, and mark up almost any surface. They drop things, fly things, and create displays of everything around them. They break apart, unwrap, and look inside things in a demonstration of curiosity. By playing with every object they touch, they display the possibility in changing forms. Forms are relocated, talked to, magically discovered—any object in the classroom can be the subject of exploration and magic.

Appropriately disguised, costumed, and made up, art teachers can assume many playful roles, introducing art lessons as inventors, magicians, or scientists. Art teachers can stack, juggle, hide, or build with pencils, books, boxes, or blocks—or anything else around. They may not be the best at these clowning activities, but they are willing.

Voice, gestures, and staging are not important if lessons are simply speeches to a captive audience. Performance-oriented art teachers, however, must analyze how they look, feel, and sound. Gestures, body movements, and facial expressions make up part of their palette. Dressing for the part will encourage further involvement by students.

Once I taught in fashionable grown-up shoes; now I wear Reeboks. My playful feet twist, jump, or improvise long shadows on the wall. In my free-fitting shoes, I can move about fancifully in the space around me, moving, building, rearranging anything within reach.

Playful Instructions

A teacher once said to me, "I told my students to draw like an elephant and no one was willing to do it." But what if we really invited the elephant to class and tried teaching him to draw? What instructions would we have to give? What rewards? Maybe if we gave him the world's biggest pencil he'd feel more comfortable. We'd have to remind him to be careful, though, because the point (and the table!) might break if he used all his strength.

Such instructions might sound funny, silly, or unusual to strangers, but not to members of a play-art class! Words are carried from one artist—the teacher—to other artists—the students—who translate them into images. This delicate process depends for success on belief, conviction, and interest—and an imaginative voice.

A lesson introduced by a talking spider, for example, advises students to choose the corners of the room that offer the most challenging drawing space for its beautiful webs. Students learn a new drawing technique, done with secret net-drawing strings (pencils on a string), and, as they experiment, discover and rediscover what drawing can be.

The creation of fantasy, the sharing of an exciting image, is more demanding than simply instructing students how to act, telling them what to do. One teacher may talk about making masks while another displays and tries on lampshades, mixing bowls, and gift boxes while giving a lively description from behind her headgear. How far will she go? How far may we go? Would we wear whipped cream? A jello-mold hat? An eggshell mask? The experience becomes one of discovering, rather than mindlessly accepting a formula, perhaps culled from some manual of tried-and-true art projects for the schoolroom.

How a teacher uses language can make a big difference in students' perceptions and actions. One teacher may say, "I brought you all this junk to work with." Another, opening a bright red suitcase, announces her discovery of famous jewels and offers to share her treasure. Both teachers may have brought in the same objects, yet only the imaginative presentation of the second teacher conjures up exciting images and art possibilities.

Hyperbolic language is useful in the art classroom. Imagining the wildest, the funniest, the shiniest, the tastiest, or the strangest in any category is a challenge for playful thinkers. Playful conversations expand art possibilities: What can art be made with? Where can it be found? What can be called "art"? What tools and techniques can be used in art? Language challenges us to reach out and try new approaches.

An art teacher who talks about incredible sights, lost palaces, or future finds injects magic and mystery into the classroom. Talk of painting with space gases or drawing with moon rocks allows students to dream of the impossible and imagine a new art. Perhaps they will be the ones to invent it!

The Art Teacher: Up Close and Personal

Students are always curious about their teachers' personal lives. Insights into the life of the artist-teacher can be a primary teaching tool. Personal stories illustrating the sources of play ideas can reinforce art lessons more than any amount of repetition.

Sooner or later, every object of interest the art teacher finds should appear in class. Reviewing the personal and aesthetic merits of each find—whether it is an old report card or a book of valentines—students learn about the visual selection process and their teacher's artistic values.

Celebrating the completion of a new painting or other work and sharing hopes for future projects can also stimulate students' appreciation of the creative process. Many students are thrilled when they get the chance not only to visit an artist's studio but to observe the artist at work. Such an experience provides even more important clues to the artistic process.

A teacher who shares information about his or her personal choices offers students an opportunity to solve visual problems. Let students see the different glasses you are considering purchasing; let them match your tie to your shirt one day. Examine together the carpets or dishes you are thinking of buying. Teachers who share their love of beautiful things demonstrate the importance they place on collecting and selecting visual items with care. Browsing through the teacher's visual world, students discover the teacher as artist and the role of art in everyday life.

The Importance of Timing

A performance should unfold throughout the class period. The teacher should visualize the lesson as a series of beautiful, exciting, or surprising events. Sequence is crucial. Let me illustrate with the story of Bobo.

When I recently brought Bobo, a mysterious monster, to class, he was packed in a strongbox fastened by a heavy chain and large padlock. I parked the package in the doorway, forcing students to climb over it to enter the room. Throughout the period, the monster mystery gradually unraveled. We began by visualizing the contents of the box. At a preassigned moment, sound emanated from the package. Later, a strong smell permeated the room. Student investigators used rubbings to uncover mysterious footprints embedded in hallway tiles. My performance changed from acting as Bobo's keeper at the start of class to heading the investigation and following clues to solve the puzzle. Later, I became the master of ceremonies for the magical rites initiating the many likenesses of Bobo created and modeled by students.

Timing is used to build suspense; its requirements dictate the sequence of introducing objects, materials, and surprises during a lesson. Each class segment may involve changes in costumes, lighting, and scenery. Objects and supplies may be unwrapped, unraveled, or made to appear magically. Work spaces may change—art that begins on a table may end up on a magic carpet on the floor or on a ship rising from the stairs. Careful timing is essential to the performance. What will happen first? What will be seen and experienced next?

One student teacher discussing performance skills complained that, although her students had responded enthusiastically at the start of a lesson that she thought was visually exciting, their interest had diminished slowly during the period. Toward the end of the class, the children moved, worked, and painted as though no significant experience had occurred at its beginning. This student teacher had yet to learn that the excitement of a performance must build through an ongoing series of playful actions that only begin at the start of an art lesson.

A play may be a brief encounter, an appetizer, before art making; it can also be the subject of an entire period. Plays can follow art or take place during predetermined pauses between art moves. How play and art are related, merged, creatively balanced, or effectively used to reflect on each other is a question of timing. Exciting plays need to be followed by equally exciting art works; timing can ensure that play excitement is carried to the art. Some plays may need to be slow and their results steadied in order to lead to more considered art decisions. Either way, play and art can, in fact, be one.

Performance Examples

Clowning Performances

The circus parade is almost ready to pull out! Last chance to check your floats! Pulling all kinds of unusual objects—from Slinkys to bells on skateboards and old pull toys—marchers select hats from our hat rack and line up behind the baton-twirling grand marshall. In the ensuing parade, each float has an opportunity to show its act as students swirl before the grandstand. Newspaper headlines shout, "Here comes the circus," their front pages crowded with pictures of our performance specialties. Doing what comes naturally, kids readily clown around. Art emerges from their performances in posters that advertise and document the circus and in the sketches used to plan particular acts. Performances also move into artworks as kids clown around while drawing, shooting pencils out of a cannon to make unusual marks or walking over art surfaces with stilts (pencils extended with sticks). We even dip spongy clown noses into paints and use them as brushes for nose painting. Themes, techniques, and objects used in a performance can be directly extended to performances on art surfaces.

Performances with Changeable Props

Students sit in a circle wearing self-adhesive papers on their faces and change expressions by adding or pulling off eyes, nose, and mouth drawings. The progress of art in any medium—the building of a sculpture, the changing of

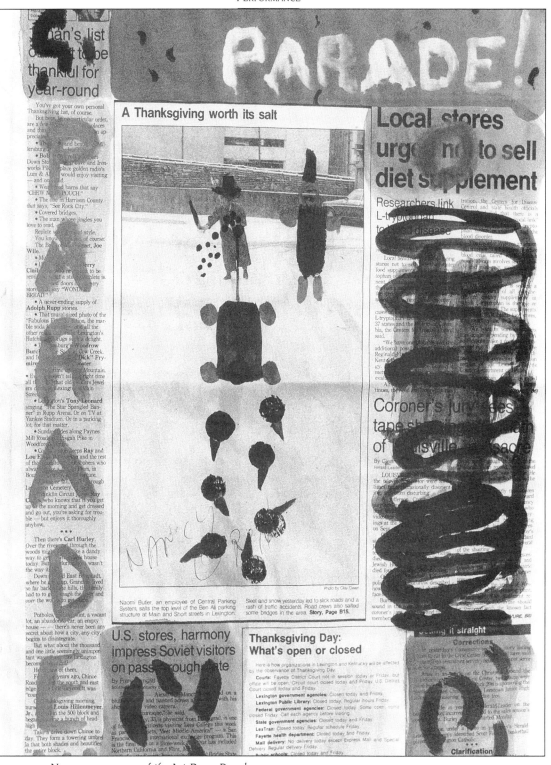

Newspaper coverage of the Art-Room Parade

forms in a drawing, and, of course, the sequences of decisions in a child's play—can be staged as a performance. Ideally, though, it should use easily shapable fun materials that have theatrical possibilities. A giant ear made of window screening and worn with rubber bands is easily flexed into many shiny shapes and decorated with unconventional earrings. The inflation of a balloon becomes a performance as the drawings on its surface stretch and change. Wires, tubes, and hoses attached to hands, hats, or any part of the body can be shaped and reshaped as the audience watches.

Remote-Controlled Performances

Put the world on a string, and think of all the objects that could be remote-controlled. In art plays, we may use laser signals, voice controls, or a variety of extension rods to manipulate forms in a performance and, later, art tools in an artwork. Fly swatters are dressed for a dance or to fan royalty. A butterfly net is converted into a giant serpent's head for a Chinese New Year celebration. A collection of unusual feather dusters kicks high in the air in a performance reminiscent of a Las Vegas floor show. In a miniature amusement park, the skeletons of umbrellas spin around tiny figures attached to their ribs. Objects attached to broomsticks, flag poles, fishing rods, or batons bounce, wiggle, and jump—dancers rehearsing to lights and sound effects. Tiny objects held in tweezers endure gale-force winds as kids fan or blow on them.

Rock Performances

From years of watching music videos, kids are less bashful about rehearsing with microphones than about performing on blank art papers. The lights, moves, and excitement of live rock performances urge them to fill art papers. Choosing from a collection of hip clothing and sunglasses, art room rock and rollers wow their audiences with the outrageous gestures and moves of rock-and-rollers that have made them famous. The acts take advantage of the vast variety of microphone toys now on the market. For example, some mikes have colored footlights; others come with sound-effect pedals built into their stands. Still others are tied to various toy instruments—sounds may come through the speakers of a toy guitar. Another group of toy mikes transmits sounds over a radio. By just adding a video camera, lip-synching sensations can easily monitor their televised concerts.

Quick-Change Performances

With wigs, large shoes, mirrors, and makeup, we bring dressing up plays into the art class. Tables are pushed together into a runway, and designers describe their new creations over play microphones. In play fashion shows, stickers on the face may start a new design trend. The latest in robot wear, featuring new motorized accessories, lights, rechargeable pockets, and self-oiling sleeves, may draw appreciative applause or laughter. Commentary on a creation by the artist or audience is an important aspect of performance sculpture. And, of course, fashion sketches and reportage can be in any medium.

Art-Room Restaurant

Food Performances

Food performing is considered an annoying kids' art form in most homes. "Don't play with your food!" is a familiar refrain as kids perform with menu items they would rather not eat. "Open the hangar for the airplane!" and variations form the text for rituals of food performance intended to coax unwilling toddlers to open their mouths for the next spoonful of spinach. Kids' creativity is especially evident in their vivid descriptions of foods they hate and how they look or would behave in their stomachs. Many early plays involve food—for example, tea parties, waitressing, or playing kitchen. These plays are well supported by the many plastic foods, dishes, stoves, and food boxes currently sold in toy stores.

This interest in food playing encourages us to set up the art room as a kitchen, to load its tables with spreads suitable for royalty, or to play with the world's largest pizza inside a hula hoop. In food performances, we use simple props such as a taped circle on a table to designate a stove or a receipt pad for taking orders from guests in a restaurant. As play menus are passed out and orders come in to the world's busiest chef, twenty dishes need to be prepared at once. In these speedy sculptural creations, we design with sponges, confetti, carrots, and staples. A child's pool becomes a giant plate for cake decorating and other messy food plays using shaving cream and food coloring. By injecting showmanship into preparing foods, serving them, setting tables, and carrying out other daily routines, we discover the performance potential in everyday actions.

Giant Performances

Enormous inflatable toys, six-foot crayons, toy playhouses, and military bases that require a van to take them home from the toy store are not unusual in the growing lexicon of children's toys. American painting, sculpture, and architecture, too, have grown to monumental proportions, as evidenced in giant hamburger facsimiles or room-size paintings. Bigger may not be better but, when we blow the world's largest bubble in class, we see that bigger is definitely fun. Scale can lift a class performance beyond the ordinary. Playing with a giant beach ball is enormously different from shooting a small marble. A life-size crayon, real or imaginary, creates marks very different from those produced with a standard Crayola. Giant objects lead to public performances and artworks rather than to private play moments. In each artwork, we can imagine searching for the largest form. As we draw on a small surface, we can imagine moving across a football field. As we work with large objects or imagine moving on enormous surfaces, we create performance pantomimes.

Children's concerns with growing up in a large adult world and their preoccupations with giants are conducive to figurative performances, in which kids may move giant forms or perform with stuffed or inflated garbage bags and other giant creations. For the largest baseball player ever, we created a stuffed garbage-bag glove that was so huge it had to be held by two players.

Performances from Art History

As the class enters, the teacher steps up on a chair and strikes a rigid frontal pose—one foot forward, the other at rest—reminiscent of Egyptian sculpture. After several poses, the class realizes that the chair is a sculptural base and the teacher is modeling changing styles in sculpture. As the demonstration nears the contemporary period, it gains momentum and soon moves off the base, just as modern sculpture is moving into the space of its audience. Sculpture today, in fact, walks—at times becoming human, doing things students in class would do. Artists pose as sculpture and build realistic wax figures, mechanized droids imitating life. This, of course, is all performable material. Art history performances let us explore both art and its history and then use our own ideas and perceptions to move from an old art to a new.

In one kind of historic painting performance, we remove canvases from their stretchers so that we can think of them as fabrics and objects. We ceremonially put these canvases through quick-paced series of performances, moving them about the room to discover their many possibilities. For example, we may place a canvas on the floor and discuss its use as a rug. We drape it between, over, and around tables and chairs and look for new supports and stretchers.

Could a tablecloth be a painting? We study contemporary paper tablecloths as design examples. Once we've draped a canvas around a table's legs, we climb inside our new tent or clubhouse and consider painting within its darkened space. We hang canvases on a line with clothespins and walk between the suspended fabrics. Could this tent become a painting? Finally, we drape the canvas on ourselves, thinking of it as clothing or another painting idea. In laying our fabric to rest, we fold it neatly over a wire hanger. But wait a minute! Could that also be a painting?

Other historical performances involve show-and-tell sessions using lunch boxes, dolls, trains, and other children's toys of historic beauty and interest. We use old and new Barbie dolls to study changes in hairstyles, fabrics, and garments in design history. The latest in contemporary toys—remote-controlled vehicles, computer-generated images and talking dolls—represent not only the future of toys but also the dreams of contemporary artists. As we look at the latest in toy design and contemporary art, we find that children and artists share a common language.

Drawing Performances

The man with the amazing stretch-a-line is our first performer. Observe, ladies and gentlemen, the act in the center ring, where our talented performer skillfully pushes, pulls, and twists the long strands of his magic gum. Each moment of this flexible performance suggests new lines and alphabets that also can be pulled over art papers.

Our next act, direct from the Orient, is a demonstration of drawing in the air. Students will perform with different-colored jump ropes to create airborne patterns. We will record this performance using drawing tools such as pickup-sticks and tracing wheels over carbon paper.

Now our snake charmers coax colored extension cords and garden hoses out of their containers. As these snakes move across the floor, they mark crossings, connections, and patterns, in ever-changing configurations for the audience to trace. Each object possesses different line qualities, weights, and movement potential that can be felt in drawings where tools are moved with empathy, responding to the original acts, sounds, movements, and waves. A twisting hose is uncoiled, a tractor chain is tied, their shadows and patterns to reappear later in artworks.

In the next act, two performers maneuver folding rulers over a line stretched across the room, inspiring ruler drawings with geometric formations and stenciled details. On the same line, the next performer uncoils twisted bands of film and recording tape. She gets so knotted up that, for her grand finale, she cuts apart the strands to wear as a piece of clothing. Everyone joins in the last act to hoist into the air a clear drainpipe with holes in it, a menacing Chinese dragon hovering over the heads of its handlers. On our papers, we capture the giant creature with big chalk marks, working very hard to keep its twisted form within the bounds of our drawing page.

Each line idea can be drawn in space, carried, displayed, walked through, and experienced through our bodies and in our hands. We capture line possibilities from performances as we experience the weight of lines, the feel of connecting them, the thrill of pulling, twisting, and curling them as we bring them into the act of drawing. We learn to make felt impressions on surfaces that we become more aware of and come to consider the drawing act as a composition and playful invention.

Painting Performances

"This restaurant serves the yuckiest foods," proclaims a sign, quoting from a review by the art room's restaurant critic. Enter the art teacher dressed as a waiter, order pad in hand and ready to go to work. Play customers sit at tables covered by white tablecloths (canvases) while play chefs await their orders, ready to mix the most unusual colors to fulfill their customers' gastronomic nightmares. Large, soft, white plates are used for mixing and displaying foods; as each becomes a masterpiece, it is carried from kitchen to tables. Disagreeable clients send waiters back to the kitchen for different toppings. Foods returned to the kitchen undergo revision and go right back to the tables.

Paint mixing, color arranging, and display can become a part of many performances. For example, in preparing the soil for a garden, we create a rich variety of earth colors. Rolling it out with different spreaders (rollers and other soil-preparing instruments), we lay out our network of rows and beds. In planting the garden, we choose from special packages of magic seeds that are guaranteed to sprout unusual colors when mixed with school paints.

Planning a garden, arranging flowers, and preparing a salad bar display, all involve arranging and displaying colors. These performances, which begin with imagination and references to real settings or use actual objects, provide opportunities for students to play with colors and to test color ideas. For instance, in a pizza-topping contest, students are not worried about painting or concerned with art but, nevertheless, are experimenting freely with unusual colors. In demonstrating our finest ice cream float and topping inventions before a convention of ice cream store owners, we create paintings but are also having fun playing with food. Using styrofoam as canvas, cups as paint containers, napkins as painting surfaces, and dipping and soaking as painting techniques, we also discover new ways of painting.

Head Dress(ing) from a Play Journey

SIX

Basic Plays

Home plays involve the creative exploration of any process and material encountered. Thus, common home plays can become an important basis for school art studies. Some of the most frequently observed plays and their art elaborations are discussed below.

Splashing and Pouring

Water lives; it flows, drips, and moves. It may be channeled and guided, blown and sprinkled with spoons, poured through funnels, squeezed through sponges, or squirted out of eyedroppers. A puddle begging to be stomped in or a child's pool crying out for some hands to paddle it may trigger exciting water play. Soaking up water in socks or on art papers or having fun at the kitchen sink with bubbles and sponges are all plays using clear, live paint—water to which color can be added. Playing with water is a rehearsal for play with watercolors.

Playing with an ice cube and watching it melt, importing snow to class, and even shaking or dangling a wet umbrella shows off water in all its changing forms. Letting water drip out of the faucet of a springwater container that has been refilled with colored water or creating showers with a watering can foreshadows the fun and freedom of blending and drawing with colors in a painting.

Young children love to be near water even when it's in a sink full of dirty dishes, because they enjoy the feel of soap bubbles and slippery forms in their hands. Just to be near a faucet stimulates imagination. Through classroom plays, we all "get into" the media: leaving hands in water, sponging art surfaces, adding colors to bubbles, mapping its descent and channeling drops of water over art surfaces.

Water in plastic bags, cups, or see-through containers can be stirred and shaken or, through the addition of various colors, transformed into mysterious soft drinks. We can enjoy the beauty of color-water blends in their containers as they line a shelf or grace a clothesline. We even study baths by treating an art surface as a tub to play in, borrowing the props and sponging actions of bath time, as well as its filling and emptying plays. We also experience rain through open windows and produce waves in children's pools set up in the art room. Still in a playful mood, children learn about painting as we channel puddles over plastics and foils, noting how the floods of color pool and disperse tracing

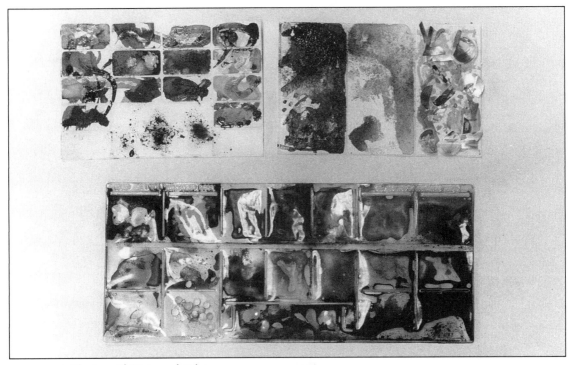

Playing with Water and Color

puddle lines we make on a sidewalk through cellophane overlays. We step into puddles and put objects into puddles of color. We get things wet both while painting pictures and while carrying out investigations of water that inspire our art reactions, ideas, and movements. Students discover that painting on paper can be as much fun as painting in a summer pool, a kitchen sink, or a bathtub.

Blowing

It is fun to blow kisses across a room or to watch children blow out birthday candles. Children discover that breathing is an invisible power from within. They delight in testing this power through mysterious sudsy gurgles in chocolate milk bubbles and in foamy puffs of bubbles in the air. They try out their gentlest blows on delicate petals and save their furious blows for stirring up storms. Looking through my vast collection of bubble makers—pipes, bubble mowers, rings, and so on—they choose exactly the right tool for blowing thousands of jewels at a time or for patiently breathing out one special giant.

In class, we sculpt bubble gum to blow beautiful bubble-gum shapes and use Chinese fans to spread colorful confetti and segments of Day-Glo thread or to reshape a freshly opened pack of Kleenex. We blow together and blow apart, blowing as a group and blowing alone, blowing separate items to form one item and blowing one item to separate into several parts. We also blow lines or shapely piles or puddles of colors together. With special blow brushes—straws or Ping-Pong balls—we blow over liquid or powdered colors. Classroom fans propel shimmering plastic sheets, ribbons, or collections of feathers. And, of course, it's always fun to watch and record the strange interim shapes of an inflating balloon figure or the unusual patterns traced around the room by a suddenly deflating balloon or beach toy.

Bouncing

Few things are more fun than bouncing on a trampoline or bouncing balls on a sidewalk. Trampolines launch bodies into space and wind them up for art fantasies. all kinds of balls in the art room become rhythmic instruments, bouncy sound makers, brushes, or printing tools as they are bounced over a variety of surfaces. To tune a pencil or brush for moving over an art surface, we stretch papers trampoline-style between tables or chairs; as pencils bounce, they absorb the sensations they experience and release them into the marks they later make. Pumping up our shoes, pillows, or pogo sticks by moving over stages, we bounce ourselves and our tools higher and higher, taking off and landing, skipping and galloping, building so much energy that it spills over on our papers.

Spinning

Spinning is a child's way of seeing the world afresh. We spin around like ballerinas until we get dizzy. We also spin like tops as we try to outperform my collection of noisy tops. To wind ourselves up, we spin our pencils—the propellers that power our art moves. Imitating an electric mixer, we spin slowly, then faster, our whirling hands serving as beaters. We listen to a tape of two world-famous figure skaters discussing spinning techniques, and, from observing ballet, we learn new names for our spins and spinning ideas. On a field trip, we go to a laundromat to watch the spinning action of the big machines.

Sorting

Kids enjoy sorting through boxes of buttons or bins of shiny washers. And, each according to his or her inner scale, they select the best from a jewelry box full of rocks, beads, and marbles. Children eagerly sort through all kinds of objects for unusual colors or textures. Recalling the pleasures of a well-stocked garage-sale table, you can imagine many possible sorting missions for your students; ask them to look for the most unusual or fashionable, the funniest or the most sculptural object. At home, there are many interesting things to sort through in kitchen cabinets, tool boxes, or attic trunks, each one showcasing related objects from which choices and discoveries can be made.

Folding and Creasing

Typically, children fold papers to make planes, hats, and fans. The paper napkins and place mats that children fold while awaiting a meal at a restaurant fill a table with sculptural variety. Even though children may not fold their towels, shirts, and blankets as neatly as adults do, their efforts win hands-down for creativity. Learning to see beauty in creases and folds, we fold large fabrics in inventive ways and research the use of creases in fashion. In ironing plays, we create beautiful sculptures and shape folds as drawings on papers. We crumple and walk over papers seeking inspiration from accidental creases. We compete to make the world's longest and most elegant folds. We study folds in the earth and create topographical and road maps or folded canals. We do all these things because creases are lines, and folding is simply a child's way of drawing and discovering line ideas.

Sticking

"Handle with Care!" "Fragile!" Stickers, stamps, labels, and different types of tapes become portable canvases to draw on, draw with, and place anywhere. As stickers, dots, and Day-Glo squares define the planes and valleys of a face structure, they form instant masks and disguises. In play post offices, we wrap packages, seal them with silver tape, then cover them with stickers and labels (our own stamps) before dancing homemade stampers over them. For more sophisticated entertainment, just enter a sticker museum featuring an exhibition mounted on the outside of a lunchbox or inside a dollhouse. Promising rock stars wear vests studded with stickers, while princes wear crown jewels with sticker precious stones. Day-Glo stickers light our way or mark our paths for plays in the dark. Ideas, messages, as art are emblazoned on Post-It bumper stickers. Drawings on tapes are flexible art that we can rearrange and piece together in playful moving exhibits.

Scraping, Scratching, and Sanding

Listen to a creative scratcher playing on a chalkboard. Can you follow and draw the tune? Scratch an old record to hear the lines made, and draw what you hear. Feel your drawing on other people's backs as you scratch their backs, and draw what you feel when they scratch on yours. All art surfaces are similarly marked or scratched as we move over them expressively. As players, we scratch and tap, making sounds over a variety of responsive surfaces. A scratched knee hiding under a Band-Aid becomes a subject of conversation and art as we make unpleasant scratches on art surfaces to be bandaged over. As champion figure skaters, we create more pleasant scratches during leaping spins and revolutions over the ice (shiny surfaces). We also scratch marks into old cafeteria trays in an incredible sound-making event guaranteed to drive everyone out of the room.

Sandpapers are some of the most beautiful papers to work with. And so we press the "on" button on our make-believe orbital, circular, and pulsating sanders. Or we adapt emery boards, nail files, and steel wool for drawing and playing over art surfaces. As we join the ranks of experienced scratchers, we become more attuned both to the sounds of art and to the pressures, rotations, and moves required to make them on any surface.

Cutting, Tearing, and Drilling

In a Shirley Temple doll case, I store a collection of favorite drawing tools: old pinking shears, barber scissors, manicure scissors, surgical scissors, tailor shears, motorized scissors, and others. Kids love to draw with scissors, leaving paths of lines they can feel, sort, and play with. Each pair of scissors makes a unique line, and through imaginary scissor plays, we test a Norwegian ice breaker—scissors cutting through northern icebergs (insulation sheets). Scissor mouths devour paper meals. Dressed in bow ties, scissors become magicians who first make paper disappear by cutting it up and then put it back together again. Racing scissors have stripes, of course, and adjustable speeds but need little fuel.

We gently use our fingers to twist and tear, leaning our bodies into tears, pulling lines down from our shoulders. Whether speedy, hesitant, musical, or twisting, each tear creates unique line impressions. Torn lines collected, traced, and traded lead into drawings. Peeling oranges or using a vegetable peeler as a drawing tool enables us to follow torn lines and piece together new edges.

Our tribal dances prepare us for earth-drilling ceremonies. We create inventive holes by boring sticks into sand or through paper or by poking pencils, scissors, or our hands into different fabrics.

Mixing

Mixers and blenders are fun to play with! Tools and students' hands can become make-believe attachments, swirling, changing speeds, and spiraling as they whip pencils and brushes into new crossings and paint textures. In our art room kitchen we celebrate the pleasures of stirring up new colors, whipping up beautiful hues in old kitchen bowls, pots, and pans. But don't lick the spoons or spatulas because our ingredients may be shaving cream and food color, sand and bubble baths. New sauces and pizza toppings are invented in our play kitchens, and distinctive toppings are served in our ice cream stores. Through mixing plays, we also develop original paint recipes—colas, detergents, sands, and grasses stirred and blended in creative ways, floated with new colors, and enhanced by unique textures.

Covering and Draping

When kids help put away groceries, they have many motives. One of these may be they just want some new headgear—usually there will be a bag that fits.

Modeling is always a joyous celebration of creativity. Kids transform themselves into squirming monsters as they are born out of blankets. With ribbons, ties, and safety pins—and the concentration of young fashion designers—they explore a basket full of fabrics. After draping their heads and bodies, they will wrap up and redesign anything and everything, from shoes to chairs. Objects wrapped in paper, foil, or plastic become abstract and easily take on new identities. Thus, wrapping is a way for children to discover fresh views or to give new functions to old forms. They even take out and rewrap our lunches, favorite toys, or hands to discover through their outer skins what their inner forms look like.

Polishing

What may be chores for adults are often magical processes for kids. Kids love the feel of drawing on a fogged or iced-up window and quickly volunteer for all kinds of polishing tasks. Applying polish then sliding on the slick surfaces is fun, as is removing dry polish to discover a shiny form. Join the fun. Put on gloves to dress your fingers as special drawing instruments for removing polish from metal surfaces or window cleaners from glass or mirrors. Such finger drawings will leave memories that can be transcribed to papers as you shift cleaning act to art making. And polishing—whether vacuuming, dusting, sweeping, or raking—develops repertoires of moves that can be translated to art. As we try out other household cleaning tools and processes as well, printing, drawing, and painting come into question.

Hanging

Standing on a stepstool (like the podium of a conductor) and hanging clothing on a laundry line can be a color-arranging challenge. Colored scarves draped from a hook and paper garments hung on clothes hangers displayed around the room become forms of play and artistic arranging. Routine household tasks are thus brought to school complete with clothes-drying racks and wooden clothespins for object-hanging plays. Hangers themselves can be balanced, attached, and performed with, and clothespins can be built into elaborate structures. Classroom closets and hangers are transformed into display canvases as children cover them with findings from laundry baskets of fabric and clothing. On a typical laundry day, rows of "flags" are hung: colorful plastic and fabric arrangements reflecting a grand-opening theme. Hanging plays move creative children's setups off desks and into room space where partitions may be hung with personally decorated shower curtains. From clotheslines stretched across the classroom we hang colorful towels to form tentlike enclosures to play in. Classroom clotheslines attached to pulleys provide movable display surfaces. Hanging from the ceiling, objects and linear materials become live drawings or space weavings to be walked through, while sheets on clotheslines become special, challenging canvases to paint on. Instead of hanging mobiles, we hang objects and strings or cords on a line to become weighted and balanced action toys. We are always looking for new places to hang things from where we can attach ourselves, our lines, and forms to classroom shades, lights, or outside trees, fences, or basketball hoop. Like spiders, we hang from corners in our webs of tapes, strings, and ribbons.

Crushing

Crushing a bug is not a pretty sight, but it is a significant ritual and science for kids who study the corpse in detail. In the school yard, we discover flattened objects and bulldoze others with bikes, hammers, and foot power; boxes, cans, and cups fall at our feet, flattened. We record each change through rubbings, tracings, or sequential drawings.

Nutcrackers help us create sculptural pileups of nuts and stones whose broken forms we study for visual changes. The powerful jaws of a squeezer smash oranges and other citrus fruit as children draw each step of the demolition. A wrecking ball—a foil-covered ball on a string—destroys card castles, Lego cities, or styrofoam skyscrapers. In some plays, we become active bulldozers, trash compactors, and garbage trucks or take part in demolition derbies, crushing papers or foils and denting potatoes or toy cars. Another very different crushing activity involves biting apples and recording their changing shapes. We also use bricks to pulverize chalks, crayons, and other items between newspapers so that we can use the resulting dust for art.

Fixing

When alarm clocks, toasters, phones, radios, and other machines and appliances break, kids love to take them apart and then to "fix" them. Fix-it plays allow kids to discover how things are made and what makes them work. Many ideas from these plays lend themselves well to art making. From their discoveries, children may come to consider sculpture ideas that tick, pop, and turn, as the worlds inside a toaster or timer suggest complex art fantasies. An old record player may be used as a revolving art stand. Each collection of dismantled forms is drawn, played with, and made into new things.

Making Messes

As muscles and coordination develop, children drop and break many things; these accidents intrigue developing minds. In the collapse of their block structures and in the chance formations of rocks, leaves, and outdoor forms, kids find unfailing art sources. Fingerprints on a clean white paper, oops! It may be an accident, but by acting on accidents, young artists use, change, and incorporate them into new discoveries. Drips on a carpet may elicit penalties at home, but in the art room, spilling, soaking, and dripping liquids is called playful staining. Accidents such as burned toast or a television set out of control simply frustrate adults but intrigue children. Unusual occasions, as well as unexpected forms and visions in the environment, are gifts to those willing to receive them. Even the miracle of a piggyback soap bubble is greeted with excitement in ways few adults ever express. This openness to change and new forms begins in children and continues with adult artists. In play-art classes, we seek to maintain both the interest and the willingness to travel beyond predictable paths and products that it represents.

Chance plays begin simply by taking a chance in art; actions and materials suggest their own extensions. Each play challenges the student to follow the sequence of new shapes and groupings being formed. Some, such as crushing, squashing, wrinkling, erasing, tearing, or cutting apart, involve taking forms apart to find clues to their reconstruction. Through these plays, students learn that all art making requires both planning and the ability to abandon plans at the right moment. Artists need to experience at an early age the fun of looking beyond safe solutions to those chance finds of interest that can transfigure art.

In class situations that promote experimentation and dispense with traditions and self-imposed limits, students can play with losing control as they gain control through each problem-solving rehearsal of an accident. Initially, chance taking can be practiced through nonthreatening plays such as seed spreading, in which students become remote-controlled dispensers, randomly dispersing seeds, pebbles, grass seeds, or marbles into chance formations. Or, focusing on melting stacks of ice cubes or tracing the crazy movement patterns of a windup toy, kids can carefully note details and record changes. By taking chances, students not only will discover new skills and new ways of creating images but also will be rewarded with artworks that are refreshingly unfussy and considerably freer in spirit than previous works.

Scavenging

Nothing in our house can be thrown out! With instinctive proprietary feelings, children stand guard, examine, and reclaim items from garbage cans. "How dare you throw this out?" is the initial challenge, followed by quick examples of how the discard could be used. With the instinct of artists and their love for found objects, children think of the garbage can as the last remaining source of free-to-claim, free-to-use surprises and true finds. And their willingness to scout the trash can, combined with a desire to save everything (from a spider web or a bird's nest to a rusty can), helps children discover important art forms without pressure.

Constructing

The Great Wall of China is really made out of cereal boxes—in my house, at least. Phone books support fluffy skyscraper cities—stacks of pillows—and

Bridge Constructed from Blocks, Rulers, and Pencils

potato-chip castles with white marshmallow towers. The bathroom boasts constructions of slippers, brushes, and combs, while large sponges peer our of their tub enclosures.

In class, we create twisting, helix-type towers out of encyclopedias and use pencils as Lincoln Logs. Eraser arches line notebook bridges constructed between desks. Chairs are balanced, flipped, and stacked into new constructions. Beginning with play examples from home and materials imported to class and combined with class objects, we learn that we can build everything and use anything as a building block. All kinds of children's blocks, from antique wood blocks to the latest block forms from toy stores, further enrich our plays. We ourselves become blocks as our hands and bodies create basic stacks, feel weights, move structures, and provide support in body plays. We never stop constructing new forms. The feeling generated is one of creative control as we empower blocks to become food in a restaurant play, telephones in an office play, athletes in a sports play, or whatever else suits the player's need or idea.

From building experiences, we begin to see two-dimensional art making as a structuring act. We construct canvases and art surfaces piece by piece as puzzles, assembling stages, screens, and drawing surfaces. Baseline drawings, which are a stage in developmental art, extend interest as students acquire a stronger sense of how to represent a floor, a base, or even gravity on a drawing paper. As kids fit things together, balance shapes and weights, and test spaces through block plays, they also relate their findings to two-dimensional drawings.

Card Playing

When you're tired of building card castles, how about playing Pasziansz? You probably aren't familiar with this game, which I played as a child, but you may have played Fish, Old Maid, or any number of other card games. Children are fascinated by the many ways cards can be held in their hands and arranged on different surfaces. Related activities with baseball cards—flipping them, trading them, and sorting them—are all part of early card playings that can be built on, either by using blank cards and card-related images and structures or by moving the play to larger planes, such as sheets of insulation materials or corrugated paperboard. In class, we have a Roladex that provides an interesting means of displaying card art (birthday cards, postcards, and other cards kids collect).

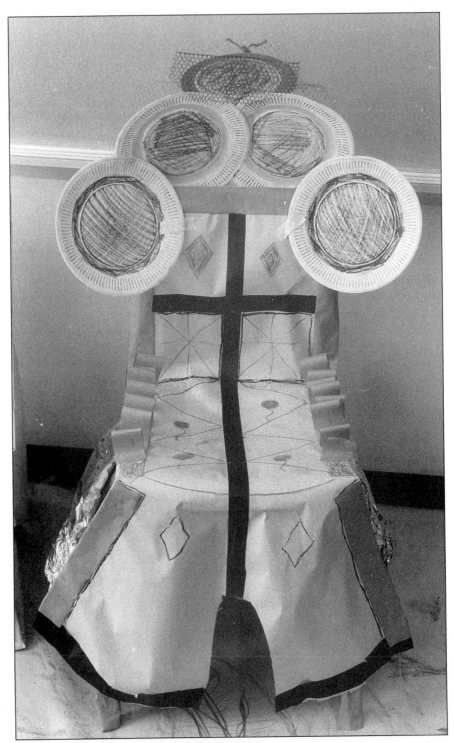

Seat of Honor for a Mystery Visitor

SEVEN

Thematic School Play

◆

Students climb over crates, slide under desks, and wear their goggles as they settle into large paper sacks. The space walk is over but the conversations it stimulated linger on. It is natural for kids who have just encountered the supernatural, touched the invisible, passed through time, and moved through outer space to dream of new experiences. One student sings the current hit "We Have the Power" while another greets everyone with the Star Wars slogan, "May the Force be with you." The class feels the power of art—they can invent, change into, or become anything.

As kids act out ideas and picture visions through playing, they enter new states of imaginary wondering. A journey may begin with masks, bags, lunch-boxes, or any simple prop. It can start with challenging tasks or unusual thoughts. It may be a royal pronouncement, an official decree to find a treasure or stake a claim that sparks playful journeys. Looking through a class trash can for treasures may lead to a new society where everyone must survive on found discards that have to serve multiple functions as shelters, utensils, furnishings, and clothing.

I once watched a young child sneaking white sugar on a piece of tinfoil. She noticed the beauty of the white crystals and was moved to play with them. In her elegant garden of snow, she placed pieces of cereal and shavings of apple curled into great sculptural configurations. With such playful approaches to environmental substances and forms, children discover art ideas most adults never even consider. A drawing surface can become sugar coated or lined with imaginary ice cream, causing students to respond with new art moves or techniques. Playing with marbles ends in discovering their potential as painting tools or as a source for observing elegant chance formations. Matchbox cars turn into exceptional printing and drawing tools, while a juicy piece of long, soft Tootsie Roll becomes an important sculpture medium. In our play classes, great sculptural forms have emerged from candy bars, toothpaste, and gum. Imaginative playing allows inventions to take form in children's most personal media. After a candy hunt, for example, students gather and arrange their collections in masterful setups. Unusual compositions abound when students play candy store, packaging, wrapping, and redesigning real and make-believe candies, using real and invented wrappings. Such openness to novel art media, techniques, and investigations lets children into art worlds denied adults.

Lessons should be conceived as visual presentations, presented through performances—demonstrations—that invite playful, creative participation. No presentation should involve students in a "follow me" type of lesson. Rather, each should be a joyful foray into a playful setting and exciting environment, using a variety of simple props proffered through creative language and playful behaviors.

This chapter describes general plays that can inspire specific playful lessons. Each was selected for its playability. The ideas are guaranteed to withstand plenty of wear or change; in fact, they are improved by being stretched and altered by anyone willing to try them out in an original way. All were tested and, indeed, discovered by children. Using these plays as a starting point, our study groups have transcended the traditional boundaries of art making and produced an entirely new range of art that questions what is or could be.

Stores

Red and orange stuffed and torn garbage bags hang off meat hooks in our butcher shop. Gum wrappers, paper clips, and rocks shine in padded jewelry store boxes. Stacked boxes are decorated as cakes for bakery shop windows. Hats are molded from unusual shopping bags and padded envelopes; vests are cut and stapled out of wallpapers.

We can set up counters, showcases, and display racks by relabeling, remodeling, and rearranging drawers, shelves, carts, and artroom closets. Suction cups with hooks, clotheslines, and hangers add flexibility to displays; erasable sale signs, lap-sized chalkboards, sale tags, labeling tools, a toy cash register, and plenty of Monopoly money foster a store atmosphere; hanging-plastic sheets become instant store windows behind which to display or tape objects.

Incidents in our store are recorded in writings and in pictures. Customers enter, to buy or to return—it costs too much; it's a bargain! Inventory is drawn, made, or drawn again. A fire sale is held. Store items are tried on, modeled before a mirror, and replaced in a display.

Playing store is a game originated by children. At one time, we all owned a shop selling pine cones, creative foods, or our artworks. In stores, display and design arts are practiced using all environmental media. Tables, countertops, trays, dishes, shelves, and windows are canvases; menus, inventory selections, and descriptions of store items are poetry; receipts, store ads, signs, and lists are creative statements. The total store—its actions, displays, and designs—is a multimedia art act. Gift wrapping is sculpting, as items are encased in papers, stickers, and ribbons. Stores produce fast-food art, extra-fancy art, ripe-and-ready art, art-to-go, and so on. Customers slip art objects on their feet, hang them from their ears, balance them on their heads, or comb them into different hairstyles.

Each store from its conception to its grand opening is a unique statement. Each one offers children an opportunity to use their design

Play Money Made for an Art Store

abilities to express their fantasies and interests: Children simply set up things they like for occasions they yearn for. In one shop, we may see a unique display of teddy bears and candies; in another, a collection of leaves and buttons for sale. Designing with real objects in imaginary stores in the twilight between reality and fantasy leads children to exciting art. Store formats also offer opportunities for the teacher to introduce students to design history—perhaps in the class antique shop, where collectibles ranging from old cereal boxes to old-fashioned toys, appliances, and hats are on display.

Food

In art class, we design menus, take orders, and arrange our food creations on tables decked with flowers and unusual place settings. Anything can be cooked!

Food Plays

Our pantries are well stocked with Play Dough, cotton, erasers, Lego pieces, shaving cream, and paper-clip toppings for extraordinary Day-Glo pasta (shoelaces). Moving outdoors, we select ingredients from sand, rocks, and leaves. Each season produces its own variety of new materials to enrich our tables. Served on colorful paper plates, stacked and displayed ingredients become extraordinary artworks.

With paper chef hats, aprons, and a variety of food-related props, food playing expands on home plays. We eat "art supplies" and other objects while documenting changes and displays. We lie down on a bed of cream (make-believe, of course) and dream of food fantasies in color—giant ice cream floats with remarkable flavor and mountain-high toppings. We sample dreams through art creations. When we tire of cooking with art supplies and other unconventional ingredients, we make art out of food, sculpting with potato chips and composing with celery and long rows of candies. Or we use funnels, basting tubes, feather brushes, blenders, or mixers to stir and spread ingredients or mix, blend, and play with colors.

We consider all kitchen experiences—from mixing yogurts to decorating cakes—as art references. When we combine, spread, or simply arrange ingredients as though we are chefs, we use techniques different from those we employ when we use a brush or knife to paint a picture. Developing a new pizza topping, for instance, and using authentic tools to spread it over a pizza shape inside a real pizza box changes the notion of painting. We think of our work as testing recipes in test kitchens and as inventing by coming up with secret ingredients. New colors become new flavors or frostings, saved in Zip-Loc bags or painted on special surfaces. Only in art class cookbooks could one find the incredible recipes executed in artroom kitchens.

Containers

Children are curious about all packaging. And in our art room, packages constantly arrive by special delivery of the art teacher. They may be eagerly searched by customs inspectors or opened during solemn ceremonies. In unwrapping plays, we close our eyes, pull out objects, shape containers, and imagine what is inside. Danger warnings are posted on some; others come with special opening instructions. We may search through surprise boxes (birthday boxes or secret trunks, for instance) for objects, instruments, or art tools. Shopping bags are kaleidoscopes where objects shift constantly as students look inside for new ideas or relationships.

We collect all kinds of containers for the art room. In flea markets and garage sales, we find old pocketbooks, lunchboxes, toolboxes, suitcases, and other property to be leased by players who will decide their uses and possibly move in. Containers can enter the class through stories, as when I showed up with a special box—it held the crown jewels!—that I had just found on a city bus. Noisy old cases lost by famous pirates, magicians, or clowns all tell their stories through labels, discarded photos, forgotten objects, or smells.

In large containers, we imagine ourselves to be in the bowels of a whale, inside a cave, or in a haunted house, appropriately decorating the walls and interiors. We design clubhouses for Pee Wee and ourselves to play in and scout out tree houses and forts, gleefully entering and celebrating inside each found container. A new garbage can can become a space capsule, run by sticker controls and pierced with windows delineated by tape that look out onto strange landscapes.

Each container has many stories, uses, and ways of being filled. Especially beautiful containers may be displayed as artworks. Others may be better suited as stages for performances or as hiding places to disappear in. Still others—the small ones—are best for providing clues or for being

Soda Machine: A Play Transformation

locked up, accessible only through the imagination. Open trunks and suitcases license us as instant manufacturers able to design and market our wares. When we take a journey—real or imaginary—we load boxes to take with us and carry along empty containers for the souvenirs that we'll gather during the trip. We make special carrying cases for toys and collections and design packages for storing unusual finds of plastics, fabrics, and papers. Containers with secret compartments, such as makeup cases with mirrors, may conceal surprise items.

Art tools may be stored in a lunchbox labeled "Doctor's Bag," "Magician's Supply Closet," or "Space Repair Kit."

For children, containers and packages are the remote outposts still under their control, theirs to set up and explore in their own way. And dressing, filling, and searching inside containers can be repeated inside art surfaces if we imagine them as containers to be filled, displayed, or performed on.

Journeys and Adventures

In our training camp for space travelers, we prepare everyone for journeys ahead. Trial lift-offs take place on a small indoor trampoline. Hoola hoops train us to endure the twists and turns of orbital gyrations. Then, lying on the floor with mirrors at our side and our feet in the air we accustom ourselves to the feel of weightlessness in an upside-down world. In every position, visual notes are entered into astronaut diaries, but art looks different. Our approach to art is different, too: To prevent drawing tools from floating away, we tied them to our space suits. Finally, we draw over inflated balloons to get used to floating and drawing at the same time.

The art room may readily be converted from a training facility to a launch site, a docking pad, or a landing strip just by adding simple markings, changing props, and rearranging furniture. Each entrance to the room can signal a surprise adventure. Instead of being planned to get everyone silently and quickly seated, rooms may be set up as journeys from school life into fantasies. Or the art room may become a time machine—a closet transformed with sounds, lights, and warning labels—to transport us through design history. Landscapes change with new names; entrances, with destination charts. We may put on a swami's turban and climb aboard a magic carpet to explore the higher views above our desks. As we close our eyes, we feel a lift-off breeze from the fan behind us. Each trip requires its own unique props and art supplies. On a carpet ride, for example, we took along such provisions as binoculars, lunchboxes, maps, and, of course, credit cards.

Leaving the marks of a journey offers many play and art possibilities. Tire marks may memorialize a cross-country auto run, while crumbs left behind as we blazed a trail through the woods may continue to form patterns over art surfaces. Walking sticks with pencil attachments can help us retrace our steps over a paper path. If it snows, the extension devices for art tools become ski poles marking our crossings over the drifts, and we are forced to draw with gloves on or to scratch messages in the ice.

In playful visualization, we go beyond school, art, and personal boundaries; we envision the ordinary then leap to the extraordinary. Each adventure results in new art discoveries over specially set up art surfaces. We take greater risks by focusing on new art subjects and inventing new art moves and reasons for making art. Through adventurous visions, we move closer to thinking as artists: we learn to look at art as a flight, a fantasy, an adventure.

Imaginary Travels Through the Art Room

Races

Up on your blocks, swimmers get ready, starting guns up (fingers in the air)! Excitement surrounds the pool area (plastic sheets marked with taped outlines as lanes) as swimmers, represented by different-colored marking tools, spring into their relay. Art is not a race or a contest; finishing first is seldom a priority. But kids enjoy action, whether racing with objects or on foot or even just watching races in a video game. Recording the play-by-play of an imaginary action or participating on paper in an imaginary race can lead to artworks vastly more exciting than those produced by slower artistic methods. Hands and tools race around, following imaginary instructions to pick up speed, change gears, or alter strokes. Drawing instruments in their fists, children might slalom down paper stretching from the classroom wall or steer their bobsleds over paper-tape runs. Or they may race flashlights, signaling turns and passing each other, and then race marks across an art surface. A pencil or brush may have multiple gears and speeds—just insert a supercharged battery or attach a flashpack and follow the countdown.

Circus Play Poster

In a society where movement means freedom, kids expect the same from their toys, videos, and artworks. Thus, we drive through art rooms and over drawing papers. Making marks from a particular starting point and moving in planned patterns and at varying speeds, constantly aware of changes in direction and movement, develops a new art style.

Parades

On a map of the classroom, we plot the many possible crossings for a parade route through the area; routes are marked with ribbons and tapes or lined with orange cones. Our parades are celebrations to which we wear hats, costumes, and signs; sounds of clapping, cheering, and marching feet order our moves. We take turns leading the march, twirling batons as we walk.

We also plan our paths and crossings when parading on art papers. Art tools follow the way of imagination as we mark our routes with confetti and note interesting crossings with ribbons on paper floors. Toys, pencils, in fact, any object can be modified to serve as an art tool and join the parade, leaving behind visible traces of the procession. Parades are a moving show-and-tell because any object or interesting find—even an artwork—can be lifted, pulled, danced with, or marched around, propelled by celebrating students.

Passing parades provide innumerable opportunities for pictures. Reportage of the circus's arrival in town features drawings of the parade. The excitement of the parade becomes increasingly apparent in our drawings as we eagerly sketch the caged wild beasts pulled by their trainers. Homemade costumes help us get into a festive spirit. Whatever we make to push, pull, or wear becomes the subject of artworks.

In live rehearsals, we synchronize our steps and then explore the beats in artworks. As horses in a parade, we prance, guided by the reins linking us to our riders, and then translate galloping into paper moves. Moving in sync or performing as links in a moving chain possesses exciting art-making possibilities. We feel our lines in action by creating parade lines, human lines of all types. We draw with joined hands while moving across long paper roads. We march and create letters, shapes, and drawings as a group, then trace our shadows. In a Chinese New Year's–style parade, we carry a giant serpent (an orange-and-black, twisting plastic pipe) decked with ribbons, tapes, and Christmas lights (which the students added)—all lines that reoccur in drawings and in paintings. In other parades, we lift our paintings into the air where they become flags, signs, and banners. As we march, we learn about moving—how movement makes lines and how lines need reasons for either joining together or remaining separate.

Dressing up

"Here is Ana!" one of the children announces to alert the family. Another spontaneous fashion show is about to begin. Ana enters, modeling her mother's blouse matched with her sister's scarf and several of her dad's belts. The announcer narrates the avant-garde features of the fashion and heralds it as the certain hit of the new fashion season. Such shows are common in most homes, as children display their interests in dressing up. Clothing plays tend to be freer than are children's explorations in more traditional art media. Dressing up creates a party—a celebration that, combined with art, allows new identities, movements, and images to be playfully explored. Dressed as clowns, children playfully juggle lines in a drawing. As pizza chefs, children apply

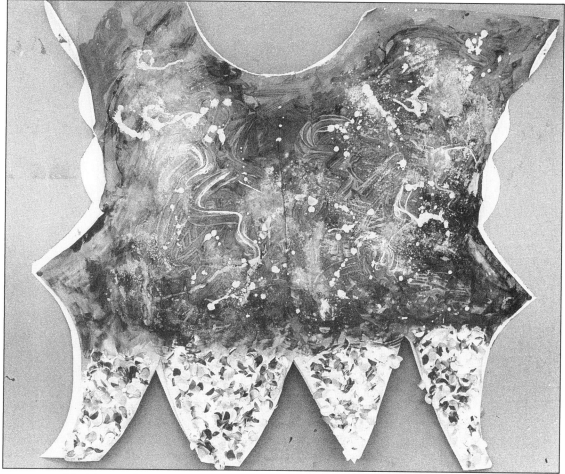

Magician's Performing Outfit

flowing colors to a painting, as through spreading sauce on a pizza crust. Getting dressed up is a rehearsal and permit for fantasy. Children take full advantage of the dynamic movements of their bodies in creating new attachments and drapings. Dressing up is a total experience for children as they play with nail polish, hairstyles, makeup, jewelry, and clothing. Generally reserved for home players, dress-up plays bring creative contributions to the art class. The primary reason for this is that as fewer art avenues remain open to children in life, fashion becomes a major source of expression and of art room explorations.

Art-room plays notice all fashion trends started by children as we further explore them and find new ones. Thus, we examine new ways of wearing familiar items, design incredible hairstyles, and present unusual ideas to fashion buyers. Classes even update the teacher's look, giving it a more "with-it" appearance.

Students enjoy it when the teacher dares to wear their creations and are flattered when the teacher models their designs. Dressing up communicates a teacher's willingness to explore unusual choices. The teacher's costume can become a signal to play, an encouragement to explore new roles and to make art differently. Artful dressing, in general, licenses fashion plays.

Clothing can be considered painted canvas; a shoe, a sculptural drawing surface. White gloves can become moving canvases or painting tools, as can old hats, which are also great sculpture bases ready for decorative treatments and extensions. Items from shirts to shorts, bathing suits, or vests can be printed, painted, or constructed from a variety of papers, cloths, and plastics. Art-made vests can be worn, and even modeled in fashion shows complete with tabletop runways, and commentaries descriptively highlighting students' ideas. Such clothing plays with found and painted garments afford students many opportunities to learn how to make artistic mix-and-match decisions. Exhibiting the results of playing with clothes simply requires imagination, clotheslines, hangers of many sculptural designs, clothespins, drying racks, and garment bags. Photo sessions with fashion finds and souvenir artworks of a fashion show may be recorded through video or other art media.

Magic

A magician casts a purple spell that not only covers everyone with purple apparel and adornments but also fills artworks with special tints and shades of purple. Purple wigs, scarves, and sunglasses further proclaim our purpleness as we transform ordinary paintings with our own magic touch. At our convention of wizards, tables display top hats with (stuffed) rabbits inside, jewelry boxes with trick drawers, and potions (candies) with special art powers. Other tables hold white gloves, old keys and locks, and streams of old scarves and handkerchiefs with striking camouflage patterns. The centerpiece is a crystal ball (a repackaged basketball). After each act, students are given what they deserve: a membership card in the Artist-Magician Union.

Art lessons build suspense as children count down, close their eyes, spin around, repeat magic words, and slow down events long enough for the magic to take effect. Magic erupts from objects and art tools as they become magic wands; art papers appear as magic surfaces to be sprinkled with enchanted powder or charmed with special incantations. We reinforce a belief both in the magic of art and in the flexible, changeable magic feel of art tools and readily transformed surfaces. Body tracings allow us to cut out and levitate creatures, saw them in half, or step out of our traced selves. Magic words and secret spells pulled out of old books are saved on wrinkled manuscript pages and placed in vaults until we can translate them into play and art acts. Colored bulbs yield the mysterious lights necessary for secret art. Magic computer drawing screens let us move images around and make them appear and disappear. In fact, art lets us do this with anything, anytime. Hair, finger- and clawprints, noisemaking mugs, singing greeting cards, and talking toys reveal the secret creatures we're hiding. Only the bravest dare to sketch the beasts.

We all have magic powers and tools at our disposal in the art room. As we look through the class collection of old mirrors, we walk through mirrors of mystery, re-visioning space and discovering detailed visions. Time machines allow artworks to change appearances, as we draw and feel changes within us. Flickering television pictures move flickering eyes toward new ideas. Remote-control devices zap things and even people onto drawing papers. What a magical way to start a portrait!

Inventing Games

Young children invent playing, making up their own rules and ways of playing and often frustrating the adults attempting to teach them "the right way." Approaching games playfully is an original kids' art that is lost if we insist that they play only by rules set by experts. But what happens when the art teacher accepts and even praises children's game inventions, allowing them to be demonstrated to others?

In our classes, we start with simple games such as marbles, jacks, and pick-up-sticks. Then we may show some traditional games and open them up for children's invention. A marble game soon requires us to shoot through dominoes and mazes, down book ramps, and around pencil courses. Each marble adventure leads to new tabletop designs, through moves that can be recorded in tracings and in drawings.

Children's game inventions are celebrated at play fairs that feature newly patented contrivances. We use pencil microphones to interview inventors, thereby affording them opportunities to unveil their game ideas. We try out all inventions, and those that test successfully are made into board games complete with instruction sheets and drawings. We learn to approach art tools playfully, preparing them for marking surfaces with the same inventive spirit that lets us devise new games. We decide how we should move across a drawing paper or make marks in a painting. Feeling free to invent, we approach ideas and problems with confidence, knowing that we can discover original solutions.

Playing with Time

One, two, three, four. . . . Ready or not, here I come. . . . When I say go, you start. . . . T—10 and counting. Counting time is used in many familiar children's

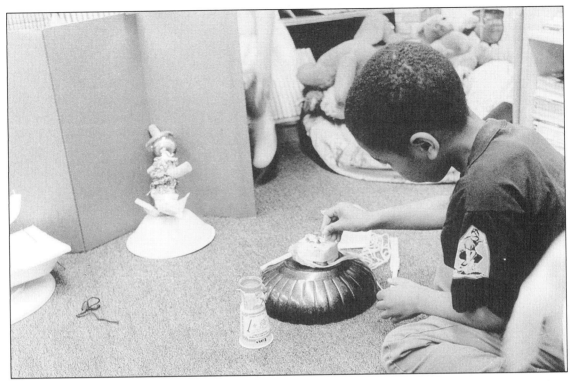

Playing with Treasure Hunt Finds

plays, for example, hide-and-seek, relay races, and space games. Even if participants in these plays cannot read clocks, they still have a strong inner sense of timing. They perceive the difference between short and long periods of time, feeling the urgency when there is a rush and enjoying the relaxed pace of leisurely time spans. When looking at art, students frequently ask, "How long did it take you to do this?" Impressed by commitments of time, they often say, "This must have taken you a long, long time to do."

In play classes, we not only talk about time but, through playful experiences, explore its relations to art. We try to meet time on friendly terms through playing, incorporating into our art making the time to prepare, rehearse, and concentrate. We play games to explore our feelings about time, to become aware of our inner clocks, and to learn to relate time to the movements, rhythms, and life of an artwork.

Instead of announcing clock time, we can develop time images by saying "Work as quickly as a hurricane" or "Draw in slow motion." Responding to such instructions, children have fun playing with timing; a deadline becomes a challenge, not a handicap. For example, asking, "Who is the fastest drawer in the West?" heightens interest in quick-paced works, while

Performance Plays

talking about a drawing lasting a hundred years makes us relax into the act of art making.

A metronome or a synthesizer can enliven time experimentation, urging us to move to different beats, exploring responses to slow and fast rhythms. Or we might listen and work to a clock's amplified ticks. During an art lesson, we can call "time out!" or work within the intervals delineated by a clock's alarm or a kitchen timer's ring. We listen to the passage of time measured by stop-watches, talking clocks, cuckoo clocks, and music boxes. We feel time by clapping it or tapping it with our feet. The teacher's purposeful actions—talking, touching, moving fast or slow—may provide a model for the class as a whole. The meaning of words such as "hydrospeed" and "laserspeed" can be communicated through actions and gestures. Signaling by hand or with signs or flags can also be a fun way to mark time.

Artists begin to create only when they gain full control over timing—when they decide when to start, pause, and stop. Art education on all levels has to train students to become aware and take charge of timing decisions over their work. Considering how timing contributes to a work is an important initial step in taking control of timing.

Light

In the still of a darkened classroom, a pattern of search lights serves as a beacon to guide a lost plane to safety. In the soft form of a make-believe cake, forty-eight abstractly arranged candles pierce the darkness. Students enjoy playing in the darkness; finding it both scary by producing plays in it and buying and inventing toys for it, they learn to create with it as well.

There are many exciting light sources to explore, from flashlight bulbs in quartz, krypton, or neon to strobe lights, black lights, halogen lights, and others. The variety in colored light bulbs, for example, rivals the most complete paint chart. Toys such as light sticks, which are glowing, portable, self-generating light sources with many optional crystal casings, provide opportunities to create drawings with light.

Controlling light sources, planning light shows, lighting specific objects and spaces, and even an occasional flickering of lights can be part of classroom lighting plays. In a dark classroom, individual light sources can facilitate exploration of color, shading, and contrasts. Playing with the lighting of a simple shape—on an egg, for example—and observing the shadows thus created enables students to experience the changing values of light and darkness and thereby understand the concepts of shading, values, and space, which are often mere abstracts in art classes. Windows can become collectors of lights and shadows—light boxes, stained glass windows, or outlets through which to observe the magnificent changing lights outside. Shades, tracing papers, doilies, colored gels, or perforated plastics can act as filters to focus and reflect colors and shades of light. A standard slide projector can be equipped with filters on the lens or show slides that have been punctured, scratched, or painted to produce interesting light effects. Photographic equipment such as flashes and reflectors can all be incorporated into light plays. Students also enjoy creating their own screens and projections using mirrors and other shiny surfaces. Shining light through hands, through pipes, or through specially designed tunnels allows for a variety of plays in passing, filtering, or blocking light. The flickering lights of computer monitors, television sets, or household timers can be used with dimmers and switches in sophisticated light shows especially prepared for the art room. Children can even record playing-in-the-dark scenes with Day-Glo crayons.

Sight Plays

Looking through giant, retractable cardboard tubes, small cardboard boxes (make-believe cameras), or plastic bug viewers, students examine closely everything around them. Homemade spectacles, mirror-lined boxes, and paper cups with different-sized openings offer still more ways to view the environment. We also enlist familiar equipment such as binoculars, magnifiers, microscopes, telescopes, and camera lenses. My collection of plastic optical sheets that enlarge, allow wide-angle views, or create multiple images always inspires playful student use; so do the truck, car, and makeup mirrors that also form part of my collection.

Sight plays help students become aware of the many dimensions of the seeing process. Squinting, blinking, and eye flickering or opening both eyes wide then closing them at different speeds allow wide-ranging exploration of changes in focus, depth, and after-image perception. We record these changing views and compare our responses to studied objects. Blocking views with hands or lenses of varied openings allows us to play with partial visions, side views, and tunnel views. Panoramic views can be studied through camera lenses and with make-believe creations such as panoramic postcards. We also capitalize on the gradual-focusing effects of special eyeglasses or blurred slide projections to play out the possibilities of various levels of visual clarity. We change our perspectives by looking through the eyes of a video camera and monitor. We pretend to see the world through a computer by imaginarily tying our eyes to it. As computers, we play with X-ray vision, interplanetary views, and sound waves that facilitate visions. Sometimes we use imaginary technology to explore impossible sights. Each new vision contributes to new art markings and imagery.

Sight plays can be combined with movement plays as we study different views of moving objects on film or consider our changing perceptions of passing people, animals, vehicles, clouds, fluttering leaves, or other transient objects. The views we notice when we stand still in front of windows and mirrors can be compared to those we see when walking or running, or in car mirrors while driving. Spinning produces altered states of seeing, not just dizziness. Students can move back and forth, over and around objects or zoom in on them to record them from up close. We even create artworks with our eyes closed.

Communication

Through the make-believe use of a variety of communication media, students observe and create images that link them to others. For example, after the familiar beep of phone-answering machines, callers respond to audio requests and messages. Long-distance calls received during art class may mean a *very long* distance, because they come from yet-to-be-discovered planets. Video-phones constructed of Legos and boxes allow visual communication from the most remote places; video cameras can assist by visually recording messages appearing on the screen.

In our art class phone plays, we try to maintain and recapture children's fascination with this machine. So, when a class phone rings, children may be answering a model not yet available at the local phone mart. Take, for instance, our Lego phones with banana receivers, which we engineered ourselves. We also try out each new toy phone as well as antique toy phones, considering these instruments as important items in design history.

And what do we do with all our phones? Well, of course, students in artist-to-artist calls talk to each other a lot, generating images and descriptions that necessitate taking messages—drawings—on a variety of memo pads. On the phone, students feel so powerful that they even call great artists of the world to share ideas. Over fax machines, students receive picture messages on toilet-paper rolls, each sheet torn off as it's received.

Students aren't attuned only to voices and images from outer space; they also keep in touch with other earthlings through secret notes and other plays. A variety of mailing plays can build on children's interests in the post office. Beautiful postcards and artistically wrapped packages may be exchanged via the mail. Stamps and envelopes are collected, redesigned, and decorated. Rubber-stamping provides further inspiration as kids create their own interesting stampers for use on stationery and stickers. Souvenir cards arriving from special imagined places are displayed beside antique picture postcards and cards with unusual handwriting in our mail gallery, located near the mail art museum and stamp art gallery next to the classroom mailbox.

For some plays, skillful images have to be created through voices and other sounds, and so we turn to radio broadcasting, which presents images and evokes imaginative communications that can be further translated into television or visual media, with their additional challenges. Ventriloquism allows students to play with voice qualities, volume, shading, and surprises as they create voice acts for artworks and other objects.

Writing movie scripts or captions for comics, videos, or artworks can involve additional play forms. Among these, narrations (including funny titles and unusual captions) for student photographs or videos can provide clues to a conceptual art language where art and language merge or language exists with art only to be imagined. Merging can be seen readily in diagram-accompanied instructions for repairing, producing, or reproducing anything and everything—even artworks. Diaries, on the other hand, usually leave art to our imaginations. In class, students elicit art images from each other by reading excerpts from their diaries, which may include personal observations about a visit to a doctor's office or the discovery of a bug.

Life Plays

Rain or snow is exciting! Playing in the snow or the rain in foul-weather gear—boots, coats, cold and wet gloves—is part of the fun. Snow can be brought into the art class and food color added to the inevitable puddles. The lines of drips and flowing water can be traced by students working under special places (e.g., wet umbrellas) or drawing with big, funny-looking gloves on. With the use of voices, videotapes, and viewers, we can all participate in important events. The winds of Hurricane Hugo were replayed in our class, blowing our art tools and papers from one side of the room to the other. Our pencils took calls as the violent winds sent them out of control. We did not leave the protection of the shelters underneath our tables until the all-clear siren sounded and drawings were complete. In 1989, we were in San Francisco during the earthquake. The feeling was hard to describe in terms other than seismographic pictures. Today, we dismantled the Berlin Wall. All of us took bricks out from the wall dividing our classroom as we celebrated by reading and illustrating the story of the Zooks and the Yooks standing on opposite sides of the barrier.

Performing Objects with Handles

EIGHT

Play Examples

◆ ◆ ◆

After viewing Juan Miró's great exhibit of paintings at the Guggenheim Museum, it was only natural for me to dream about what it would be like to have the young Miró in one of my classes. What could I do to teach him?

To inspire his sense of visual humor, maybe we could become clowns. He would enjoy making up faces, dressing up in unusual costumes. To inspire his sense of material inventions and foster his excitement about shopping for material ideas, maybe the classroom could become a flea market. I am certain he would also be interested in all the prizes in a bubble-gum machine. To encourage feelings for creating vast, open spaces with lively movements, perhaps the classroom could become a playground where he could enjoy hopscotch and cat's cradle, trying out gestures in plays as well as with paint. Searching for timeless forms, he would surely enjoy digging in the sand or blowing outrageous bubbles. To meet the needs of the great future artist and prepare his hands and spirit to play freely and inventively in art, I would have to work hard to promote all types of playing. My classroom could not offer play environments less great than those found later on in his artworks. I would need to satisfy young Miró's thirst for experimentation, to show him the fun of finding new worlds.

We can't look at Miró's works through ordinary eyes or come close to them with everyday spirits. Neither can we teach a future Miró in an ordinary schoolroom with only traditional approaches. It is by becoming a juggler or experimenting with magic and exploring the possibilities of playfulness that we're able to visualize shapes, fantastically march across a class, or wear colors that imaginarily launch us on space flights. Aren't these the joys, the fantasies, and the dreams that Miró's paintings speak of?

Playful and experimental environments created through words, actions, and simple setups support and involve kids, allowing their creative acts to surface in the purest form. This chapter describes and reflects on actual plays, set up in public-school classes, that have achieved this goal. In each, the attitude is one of looking ahead: playing to discover art. Each play is a search, an engagement in a poetic act; each illustrates how art is an accessible part of children's lives.

Food Plays

Everything was all over the place yesterday—mustard, catsup, and horseradish squeezed out of their handy little packets, dropped in rich, thick beads onto

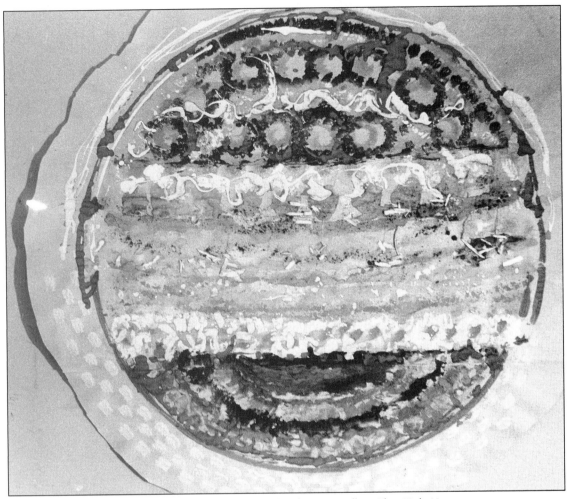

Toppings for the World's Largest Pizza Painted with Tennis Balls Inside a Hula Hoop

paper plates, napkins, and fast-food containers. It was just another art medium the children had discovered (and gone all out to explore) as they mixed their paints and coated every available canvas in a fast-food restaurant.

Details often have to be changed when plays are imported to class. In this case, colored napkins supplemented those of standard white to allow for a greater variety of color experiments. A second artwork—a painting of the paintings—provided a permanent record of the nonpermanent play, since kids could not bring all their catsup pieces home.

The first paintings were filled with many inventive ideas as well as a playful spirit and setup, which we tried to maintain in the second artworks. But our second artworks were not copies; they were new inventions inspired by play finds. We kept the restaurant-related canvas choices (napkins, placemats, and fast-food boxes) but refilled the packets with more permanent paints—the class made great mustard, unusual catsup, and original horseradish. In addition to the refilled packets, there were choices of dabbing brushes (e.g., Q-tips and leather-tanning daubers) to simulate and extend plays. Adding a little bit of the real thing—catsup, Kool-Aid, Coke—to the school paints helped to maintain the playful spirit of the original act.

Derby Day and Beyond

The teacher models beautiful bonnets and straw hats from the twenties through the fifties. Even though the children are immediately interested in the unusual hats with their flowers and fancy ribbons, they laugh as the male teacher and principal player models them.

I am becoming a Kentuckian, not because of a growing expertise in horses, but because I increasingly feel the special excitement of Derby Day. Students also catch Derby fever as I tell them about a very special race I attended in my home: A pink little pony was first at the finish, jockeyed by G.I. Joe; a much bigger stuffed horse with wings was next, with Barbie in the saddle; the third post position was held by a My Little Pony ridden by a robot. Borrowing props from this very special derby, the class begins to set up its own track, beginning with the starting gate, a piece of folded, printed cardboard—part of Barbie's rock-star backdrop. Deciding on a slow track, we use an oval-shaped table over which we lay brown wrapping paper, slightly creased and sprayed for wet spots. To ease tension before the race, we visit the Derby Museum to admire the variety of old toy horses on display (one a horse with a clay rider that I played with as a child). We also bone up on form by studying a book about metal toys—including wind-up horses and tin race sets.

A toy cap pistol starts the race, and horses begin to move furlong by furlong around the room, passed from student to student. Hoofprints mark the track, and the fast-paced action is recorded by the fans. Action called over a play microphone passed around the class paces the contest and promotes closer observations. As the horses make their way around the track, varying views are offered, from close-up to distant. Some children draw from the perspective of the rider; others, equipped with four tools, imitate the galloping horses.

Everyone Loves a Circus!

As students enter the classroom, they pass tables that have been pushed to the side and see, spotlit in the center ring, a self-standing cage (chicken wire) decorated with flags. Big animals, waiting to be tamed, pace restlessly inside the many colorful, covered laundry-basket cages that also litter the ring. In the prop room (a labeled table in the corner) are the hoops, stands, balls, and other items that tamers will use to enhance their wild (stuffed) animal acts. Animals are auditioned and props tried out in playful rehearsals. Leaping and balancing acts, waterfall routines, and numerous original performances are applauded by

Rehearsal in the Circus Ring

a gloved audience. (All kinds of gloves—surgical, hunting, gardening, and others—are available from the glove-collection box.) Gloves become quick-responding paint brushes with which to record fast-paced acts. Hand-animated art is followed playfully by glove-animated art, as we challenge our painting gloves to roll over, jump, growl, and actually perform on paper.

Swinging with the Times

Students dressed in white canvas (folded paper with neck openings) turn and twist, showing front and back to their equally well-dressed, canvas-wearing partners as they rhythmically draw on each other and to the music. The fast, Latin rhythm encourages invention as moving artists meet moving canvases, resulting in a playful display of rhythmic lines. The teacher, wearing a sombrero and marking time with maracas, sings and dances alone among the dancers to help keep the mood.

Later, dancing canvases are transformed into rock stars. Red microphones are set up as students browse through a collection of rock tapes. On one table (labeled "Instruments for Rent"), toy guitars, synthesizers, noisemakers, and other sound producers are available for selection. In a corner labeled "Dressing

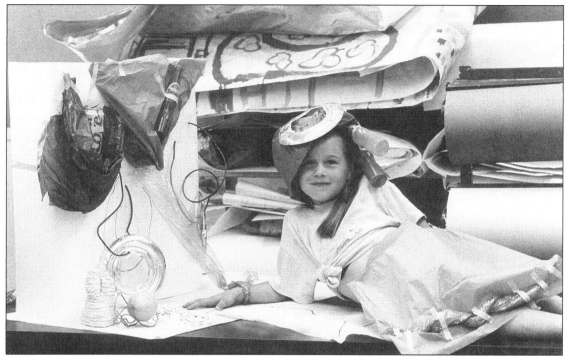

Modeling the Latest in Fashion and Accessories

Room," disguises abound, such as old Hawaiian shirts, a selection of wild hats, and plenty of jewelry, sunglasses, and gloves. There is also a choice of instant makeup, including stars and dots (stickers) and camouflage paints. When ready, performers check their finery in one of the several full-length mirrors provided for the occasion.

As spotlights (flashlights) hit the rock groups, playing and art become inspired and flow more freely. Each group performs the new moves it has developed to go along with its instrumental and sound improvisations. Fans follow along, teaming their art tools with the new moves. We all sing, clap, and move together as we watch live performances on art stages. Students further respond with energetic marks, altering and adding music and move-ment notations. To keep the beat, to strum and drum along, we dip pick-up-sticks, chopsticks, toothpicks, and long matches into inks and tap our way across papers.

Beastlike Tools

Funnels of all sizes and colors are set up on one table. Folding rulers of all ages and discolorations fill the big, red Sears toolbox on a second. In-side kitchen drawers lined with pretty papers is a collection of old and new, unusual kitchen utensils, making the third table look like a kitchen table on cleaning day. Staplers, pliers, clamps, and other beastlike tools with moving features sit on the last table. Players are invited to open up, try out, test, animate, and motorize their finds, to name them and introduce them to each other—in short, to do whatever the objects suggest. Funnels are traced and made to perform in different acts. Some folding rulers become animals; others, caricatures and monsters with wide-open mouths (when pliers are added). We play with objects to discover ideas. We can give any object a new identity and transform it as it changes us. While we carefully position and inspect an object so we can trace it, we think of others and the related forms they suggest. What would be the funniest, wiggliest, wildest thing to tame and trace? Rubbings, wrappings, videos, and, of course, tracings help us hold onto things, keeping them still while we study and learn from them. We use promising objects—interesting, open forms with many possibilities—instead of educational toys or art supplies. Tracing isn't scary; it's a fun way to collect forms and ideas while freely adding our own touches.

On-Track Creativity

Not long ago, I told my students about Kleinbahn, my thirty-year-old train set, last played with (mostly under my bed) in a one-room apartment in Vienna. As I ceremonially unpacked the train one item at a time, I explained that my parents could afford only the basic set, but that using shoe boxes for stations and sponges for ramps, I had invented a more complete setup, all the while wishing for a railyard, a set of semaphores, and a track system to reach around the world. The children understood my dreams, and soon we were all on the floor, intent on realizing the vision of a great train layout that I had fantasized about all those years ago in Austria.

Starting with lots of floor space, we extended the available tracks with adding-machine tape so that we could crisscross them over the entire floor. We wrapped and redesigned a big plastic soda bottle as a water tower, and a series of clear cups placed on a see-through box to form a modernistic series of rivets (stickers) and fastened to a moving platform (skateboards) became a refueling and watering stop for big steam locomotives. From a pile of mechanical switches, pumps, transformers, and springs, an elegant ultramodern train-repair yard became operational, manned by G.I. Joe figures. From gutter parts neatly lined with rows of shiny tapes and reflectors, we constructed the three-piece tunnel of my dreams. And from hair curlers and Christmas lights, we built semaphores with working parts. The rail controller monitored traffic from a video screen (an Etch-a-Sketch), while a series of interestingly shaped folding rulers blocked car traffic from the tracks. The construction's progress was mapped and videotaped by students.

Later, we created drawings that followed our eyes (and noses) close to the track, recording the moving views of train passengers and crew. Other

Toy Train Repair Yard

drawings emanated from a screen as the rail monster in the control tower followed the train's movement. Sitting backward in helicopter seats (our chairs), we flew over the tracks to draw aerial maps.

Architectural Finds

In art class, we begin by surveying the room, checking for good lots to build on, favoring those with interesting ledges and views (e.g., on windows and chalkboards) and other exciting features. Rolling shelves, open drawers, and corners are claimed, and building permits issued. Evaluating the features and faults of each site is a part of play conversation. On the computer (or magnetic sketch boards), preliminary building ideas are projected, and proposals presented to property owners or town councils.

Students begin browsing through the latest construction materials—antique blocks, bricks, stones, and other building materials. They even find leftover Halloween candy, enough to build an elegant candy villa. Additional treasures include hair curlers, PVC pipes, combs, and stackable baskets that can be transformed into structural accessories. Challenged not only by the interesting media but also by the freedom to select and test them, students combine

Cake for a Birthday Party

wood blocks with Legos and golf balls, as well as other novelties, to erect their dream structures: homes, forts, and monuments—even entire cities. Some structures lean over a table's edge; others span chairs or rise from a trampoline-and-swivel base. An umbrella becomes a stadium dome. Each play yields many drawings of the site, construction progress, interior views, and ads and realtor walk-throughs, created on art papers (graph paper, old blueprints, vellum, and insulation board) with stickers, tapes, labels, and rubber stamps to simulate architectural elements on paper. Students observe blocks; light them; and study them from different distances, heights, and angles.

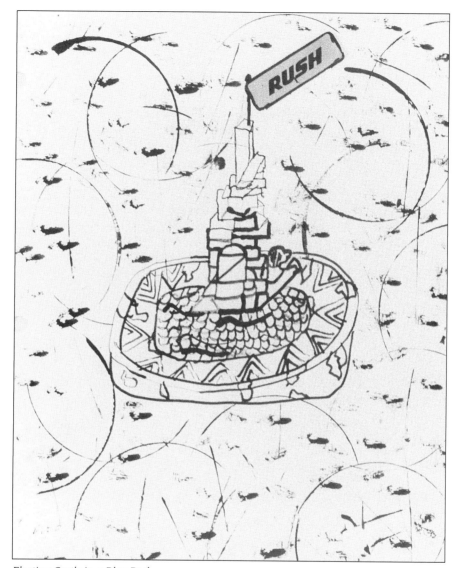

Floating Castle in a Play Pool

Pooling Ideas

With buildings (stacks of chairs) in the distance, three round swimming pools occupy the middle of the room. The Mediterranean Sea (the first pool) is filled with sunlight (a light source) and blue water (food color), edged by bright towels sporting unusual sunglasses and even bottles of suntan lotion. In this relaxing scene, we enjoy the sun and build our floats of fancy wit tub blocks, silver insulation board, and shiny, white foam plates.

Our second pool is isolated by orange cones and a construction sign. Floatable building materials stacked in piles are ready for use in bridge construction. Meanwhile, huge traffic jams (of toy cars) line each side of the bridge.

Our third pool, larger than the other two, holds distinctly dark green water. Plastic and copper pipes in triangular and straight configurations (which obviously don't float) await the designers of an underwater palace. Swim goggles, a map, and a storybook at poolside alert viewers to the presence of underwater players before their descent.

Projection Plays

On a large classroom screen of paper, creatures run rampant. Using our slide projector as stage light, we begin our plays in the dressing room, where hands and/or feet find attachments such as gloves, tweezers, springy

Object Shadows Transformed into Characters

feet (Slinkys), and expandable jaws (nutcrackers), among other things, to animate. Objects are tried out in various ways—taped, combined, juggled, hung, and traced–as they are projected onto the screen or playfully captured on paper. Some creatures swim around in under-table tanks as they are traced inside a light box (i.e., a table with its legs wrapped in tracing paper to conceal shadow performers). A projector (equipped with extra-long cords) enables us to throw images onto different surfaces (walls, corners, blinds, and ceilings) and explore new projection angles along with focusing and size plays. Eventually, our bugs become specimens to scrutinize under bug viewers or on slide mounts made from miniature drawings that we have created by reducing our large-scale tracings. We draw, scratch, white out, and paint (with nail polish, water-colors, etc.) over blank slides then project the new slides on the original paper screen, adding many new insects to our wall chart of newly discovered bugs.

Button, Button . . .

The lid to a rich-looking button box opens, inviting players to browse, sort, and display. We choose our game boards from among a selection of brightly patterned paper tablecloths, gift wrapping, and graph papers then add tracing patterns to buttons, surrounding them with imaginative stories (the King of Buttons, I am told, always wears a smile—drawn over round stickers—while in the button palace, where brightly nail-polish-painted button art hangs). Our antique-button museum is housed in a small, glass box with many spare compartments for the new finds curators are always uncovering. Since each piece represents a distinct period, just as do the clothing items from which they were clipped, our painted enlargements of button exhibits let us review design and painting history.

Memorial Day Parade

On Memorial Day 1990, white paper rolled along the tops of art room tables marked the parade route. Children's lunchboxes served as review stands and storage boxes for miniature participants—Smurfs, California Raisins, transforming robots, and marchers found in Happy Meal boxes. Some marching units were set up in playful formations, while others lined the streets to watch the parade. With stickers, Play Dough, and voices, children enlivened the scene, providing marchers with new instruments, signs, applause, and sound effects. To add movement to the parade, students pulled the marchers along on paper, creating a conveyor-belt effect.

In the second part of the parade, we explored marching rhythms using all kinds of rubber stamps (and stamp pads) to march across art papers. Finally, children videotaped the parade, marching alongside while drawing, and fashioned sculptural wire sketches.

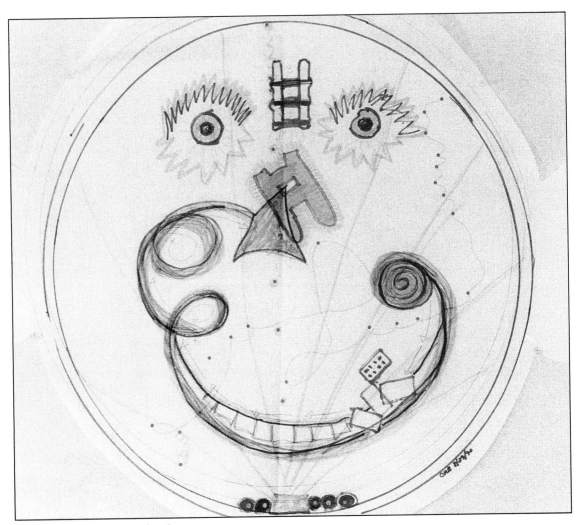

Marble Play Obstacle Course

Marbles and Such

I set up black and silver targets on a classroom floor covered with white paper and pattern the floor with colored hoops to serve as arenas for great marble games. I pull colorful, shiny, see-through shooters from cloth sacks as the kids sit around the circles and await their turns to play. I shake another sack and listen to its contents as I pour out its surprises, forming new configurations in the rink. Each spill introduces a new marble, which, in turn, becomes a rolling sculpture, with exciting patterns constantly repositioned.

"Not many new marble games have been invented lately," I tell the class, recounting the games I played as a child. Thus challenged, from our construction box, we pull out dominoes, playing cards, and Legos to assemble marble ramps and runways and to design shoots, obstacle courses, and golf games adults have yet to consider. Pencils become bats and cue sticks, while funnels and hand mixers launch, crank, and mix marbles and blend plays. Marbles shot against golf balls knock Ping-Pong balls into new positions, thereby altering colors and patterns.

It helps to put the art surface right under the action, so that little time and interest are lost in recording play ideas and events. Children draw the track, trace the roll of the marble, mark special instructions, and paint the most beautiful pieces. Rolls, ricochets, crash marks, and hits are all part of the game and part of the lively drawing act. Fast-marking, roll-top shoe polish, nail polishes with glitter, and transparencies help players capture the fast-paced marble action.

As part of marble dreaming—visualizing the most colorful, unusual, largest, most sparkling, and otherwise special marbles—we look through a new colorful history of marbles. Then, thinking beyond present play objects, toy inventions of the future, and whatever else may be possible (or impossible), students dream on in other areas. Marbles bring their expressions, moves, bodies, and spirits alive on and off the art paper.

In the Great Outdoors

For one of our many outdoor walks, we went to Ashland, the Kentucky home of Henry Clay, a historical home surrounded by sweeping lawns and formal gardens. On entering the brick-walled formal garden through the wrought-iron gate, we formed a long line and began winding down the paths, each of us following the canvas (paper) taped to the back of the person in front. From the window of our slow-moving sight-seeing tram, we recorded all the sights. Challenged to draw from start to finish, left and right, our eyes took in everything as we moved along. Whispered conversations traveled up and down our line as messages were passed back and forth between the crewman in the caboose and the engineer up front.

Instead of moving to a single site, we playfully explore the entire space first, getting a sense of its whole. Children collect their supplies on site, picking up perhaps the smallest or most precious things they can find. They have brought along souvenir containers—shopping bags—for their finds. Initial expeditions may yield sticks, flowers, needles, and stones, which kids use to set up and arrange their garden plot within the garden. One student found some little black pebbles that we began to think of as magic seeds. Planting them, we envisioned flowers never before grown in Ashland.

With a bubble blower in hand, I tell about the little girl I met blowing bubbles in Mr. Clay's garden. Unfortunately, the bubbles grew so large that they wrapped themselves around each tree and flower and even encased the visitors' heads in clear helmets. Student response was typical—the children told an even better story. A giant magnet in the sky, a student explained, turned even

Play Arranging of Outdoor Finds

the biggest trees upside down, uprooting everything with its pull. As we continued fabricating visions, we actually saw Henry Clay himself (1777–1852) dining in the garden, waiting to pose for us. Of course, we recorded our visions and stories as another form of play, realizing that we were not meant simply to copy things but rather to respond imaginatively.

Our outdoor canvas took advantage of the vast scale and encompassed even the extensive lawns. Using white yarn, we drew trees as big as the old oaks. Springing from the roots of their originals, our trees looked like giant white shadows. With colored surveyor's tapes and flags, we enlarged the flowers into giant groundworks, exemplifying the big moves, big ideas, and big plays that the outdoors can inspire.

Because it was a hot day, we had brought our own watering cans to water the plants. Spills marked the concrete and brick walks with original water drawings, which we sketched on paper before they evaporated. We then wetted large sheets of papers and continued the play by recording it with our watering-can brushes, now filled with colored water.

The garden is noted for its well-manicured shrubs. One player proudly announced that she is allowed to help at home by using a hedge trimmer. I mentioned that I had brought along a motorized version and, with an appropriate sound effect, pulled some scissors out of a tool box. We knelt before each bush and shrub in the garden and proceeded to tear and rip its likeness in paper. When we had created a sufficient number of paper shrubs, we went on to trim them. As our shapes grew wilder, changing into bugs and monsters, we noticed how real trees, too, could resemble people and animals.

We used our imaginations to climb right to the top of a tree, where we sketched surrounding views. Afterward, we went inside a tree and let ourselves be carried by its sap from the basement (roots) to all floors above. Play talks, gestures, and pantomimes opened all doors as we met and drew (with grass clippings and dirt) the creatures that lived inside and out. Before we left the park, we said good-bye to the trees, hugging and dancing around our favorites, then limply swaying to communicate with them in their own language.

Shopping Sprees

During a trip to K-Mart, each student became the expert on an aisle and guided the others through the object finds. According to one guide, tennis racket handles had faces that appeared in different portraits. The digital scale was really a time machine. Doctor Scholl's foot pads were stamping aids. An egg slicer in the next aisle was a clay tool, while Band-Aids became canvases for nail-polish art. Golf balls, tennis balls, and basketballs in still another aisle were referred to as rolling brushes. Plumbing parts were play blocks, and different kinds of plastic bait made great printing tools. Discovery promoted artistic confidence as shoppers dared to think of building, drawing, or painting with anything on any surface. We left K-Mart with lists of ideas, plans, and possibilities that we couldn't wait to try.

Touch and Tag

Touch and tag interesting objects in the room. Lay them down, tilt them, stack them, or twist their necks in playful touching and placing to discover new possibilities. Circling around the room, we rediscover ordinary objects—lights, chairs, a paper trolley, a fire extinguisher, garbage cans—through touch. All are duly tagged with Post-its bearing students' names.

Let's try wrapping our objects as big presents! Children browse through boxes and other containers, searching for just the right combination of wrapping in the choice of unusual foils, gift wraps, plastics, ribbons, laces, and tapes. Afterward, we admire all the well-dressed objects, new canvases for our imaginations to play on.

Kids test, try out, and discover everything. Playful circulating—walking backward, spinning, blinking, looking down, and walking with flashlights—generates new ideas. We speak of motorizing, pulling, and floating objects, of living inside them. With some magic words and through hard play, we discover special clues in ordinary, wrapped objects. A table wrapped in plastic becomes

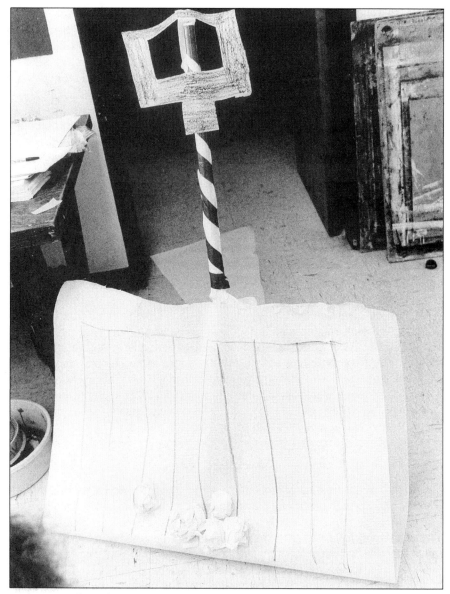

Making Items for a Play Store

a fish tank; wrapped chairs, a drive-through window; a shelf, a condo; a garbage can, a space capsule.

We paint from our wrapped presents, exploring the new images inspired by the wrapped and tagged forms. Using long sticks (such as bamboo, broom handles, fishing rods, and vacuum-cleaner tubes) with brushes taped to them, we create clear, large-form studies without fussy details. Before the painting starts, we raise our tools in a player's pledge to keep playing through each step of the art and not simply to copy previous play.

Play Horse Portrait

Epilogue:
Teaching Ideas

Art teaching in the future must be creative to foster creativity; it must set aside art—what we know as art—to allow students to dream beyond it. Only then will players learn to see art in the most open terms. When posed as creative experiences, even the most complex art problems become playful challenges. Art lessons become hopeful experiences, rather than obstacles to be surmounted. But, as teachers, we must develop and present the ultimate plan for each session: optimum opportunities for independent investigation that will provoke students to take the first—and most important—step toward gaining control of their art. At the same time, we must remember that our art rooms are filled with children, not art students. The following suggestions may make it easier for us to achieve these goals—and easier, as well as more enjoyable, for students to reach their own.

Make room for children's interests

- Move from sandbox play to earthwork design and creation, from water play to watercolor experimentation, from block plays to architectural designs and construction, and from dollhouse setups to the interior design of community- and personal-use spaces.

- Learn from children's rhythmic moves along sidewalks: straddling, walking on, or avoiding cracks; jumping fire hydrants or puddles; skipping or swinging around trees, light poles, and friends. All of these playful movements can be transferred to art surfaces through art tools, which merely extend our bodies.

- Invite children to gather, package, and share (through show-and-tell) their found treasures.

License children to play

- Through signed statements, guarantee all players the freedom to search for individual solutions, seek the outrageous, consider the unusual, and think the unlikely.

• Use supportive phrases, such as:

— "You're free to play in this room; just enjoy your playing."

— "Don't worry about what your play [or art] is supposed to look like; trust your intuition and have faith in your ideas."

— "Play out every possibility you can think of—just see what happens."

• Demonstrate playfulness regularly and welcome similar gestures from others.

• Encourage children to see the environment as a resource by allowing them to play with everything in the art room. Demonstrate some of the ways things can be touched, moved, or transformed.

Create opportunities for play

• Using simple words, invite children to enter a haunted house or castle, land on a treasure island, or visit a junkyard.

• Through creative setups, transport children anywhere they can imagine in space and time.

— A child's pool becomes an ocean.

— Flashlights light a long, white-paper runway for an incoming plane.

— Art room designs promote safaris or treasure hunts. Remember to fantasize freely and to think about unusual settings before either connecting them to a plan or considering materials. Remember, too, that children involved in someone else's fantasy still need opportunities to search for their own.

• Rotate physical settings—new places, surfaces, or spaces—to elicit new play starts.

• Replace seating plans with ushers and travel guides; trails and runways; and paths with obstacles to drive or crawl through or to hop or jump over.

• Introduce playful behaviors by engaging children in exaggerated humorous conversations, by posting imaginative signs, and by providing creative instructions.

• Use the power of suggestion to generate heat, cold, light, darkness, and the like, as well as to create an urgency for relief or satisfaction.

• Encourage touching, which is a basic means of playing and of conducting an artistic search. In essence, drawing and painting are sensitive touching processes.

• Rehearse creative states.

—Invite children to invade paper space with easy-to-erase sketches, drawing with flashlights, sand, or straw.

Encourage discoveries

• Deputize everyone in the class to look for interesting things, perhaps the latest treasure from anywhere.

• Demonstrate personal excitement and curiosity in harvesting new finds.

• Promote auditions of objects through plays to facilitate discovery of the objects' latent abilities and talents. Use different plays to explore a single object or material. (Present plays in steps, with each act either building on the previous one or contrasting with it.)

• Pose art lessons as questions that challenge children to investigate and discover.

• Provide opportunities for active discovery involving the selection, collection, and trading of raw materials with which to work, then design lessons to promote and enhance selections.

• Encourage student participation in preliminary shopping, browsing, visualization, and rehearsal by preparing old picture files, shopping bags, sticker books, or tool boxes.

• Praise students for daring choices and for going beyond obvious or readily accessible materials to seek new, surprising possibilities.

• Set up plays that provide opportunities to look for art clues—for example, test sites, test kitchens, or wizards' workshops.

• Introduce color mixing, shading, and perspective, in nontraditional ways that lead to personal discovery. (For color mixing, use mixers, blenders, or eggbeaters; for shading, in a darkened room, shine a flashlight on a white egg or on white blocks to reveal their shadows and three-dimensionality; for perspective, use cardboard tube viewers to scout toy setups at a distance.)

Foster independence

• Respond to students' investigations by listing and praising each independent action and by summarizing independent choices.

Add drama

• Produce light and movement plays.

• Arrive in class with, for example, packages containing sounds and moving objects, unexpected items inside unusual containers, or creatively wrapped gifts (for birthdays or unconventional holidays).

• Throw a surprise birthday party with all the trimmings.

Capitalize on the outdoors

• Encourage freer movements and large-scale designs to create temporary drawings or sculptures using, for example, bricks, corrugated drain pipes, and floor tile in colorful arrangements.

Use creative timing to sustain student interest

• Alternate slow and fast-paced activities.

• Introduce new materials, work spaces, and play experiments at unexpected moments.

• Time performances.

Along with having fun, students must learn to associate art class with seeking art and ideas—instead of with receiving them. The ultimate goal of art learning is art making without the teacher.

Works Cited

Almy, M., P. Monighan, B. Scales, and J. Van Horn. 1984. "Recent Research on Play." In *Current Topics in Early Education* (Vol. 5), edited by L. G. Katz. Norwood, NJ: Ablex.

Association for Childhood Education International. 1988. ACEI Position Paper: "Play, a Necessity for All Children." *Childhood Education* 64 (3): 138.

Bohrer, Michael. 1984. *Mummenschanz*. New York: Rizzoli.

Fein, G. 1986. "The Play of Children." In *The Young Child at Play*, edited by G. Fein and M. Rivk. Vol. 4, *Reviews of Research*.

Francks, Olive. 1977. "Genesis: The Art of the Young Child." In *Early Childhood*, edited by B. Persky and L. Golubchick. Norwood NJ: Avery.

Hedgecoe, John, and Henry Moore. 1968. *Henry Moore*. New York: Simon & Schuster.

Klee, Paul. 1967. *Creative Confessions*. New York: Praeger.

Mandelbaum, J. 1987. *Young Children*. New York, Random House.

Moyer, Joan. 1989. "Whose Creation Is It, Anyway?" *Childhood Education* 66 (4): 16–22.

Piaget, Jean. 1932. *The Moral Judgment of the Child*. New York: Harcourt Brace and World.

Read, Katherine. 1980. *The Nursery School: Human Relations and Learning*. Philadelphia: W. B. Saunders.

Sheehan, George. 1980. *The Running of Life*. New York: Simon and Schuster.

Winnicott, D. W. 1924. *The Child, the Family and the Outside World*. England: Penguin.

Bibliography

• ◆ •

This bibliography is an inventory of the books used in our play laboratory. Books are an important part of the program. Some are used by teachers to learn more about children, their play, and their art, while others are beautiful creations to share with children so that their play discoveries light a path to the appreciation of art.

Theories and Background

Almi, John. 1988. "Basic Human Values for Childhood Education." *Childhood Education*: 64 (3): 4–8.

Axline, Virginia. 1979.*Play Therapy*. New York: Ballentine Books.

Barrett, L., B. Corsaro, J. Isenberg, and V. Suransky. 1982. "Play: Practical Applications of Research." *Phi Delta Kappan* 5 (1): 1–4.

Brodus, Katherine, and V. Lauren. 1987. *Play Is Not Just for Kids*. Waco Texas: Word Books.

Cherry, Clare. 1976. *Creative Play for the Developing Child*. Belmont, Calif.: Fearon Press.

Franks, Olive. 1986. "Genesis: The Art of the Young Child." In *Early Childhood Education*, Ed. B. Persky, pp. 45–51. New York: Avery Publishing Group.

Gardner, Howard. 1973. *The Arts and Human Development*. New York: John Wiley and Sons.

Isenberg, J., and N. Quisenberry. 1988. "Play: A Necessity for All Children." *Childhood Education* 64 (3): 11–14.

Leiberman, J. N. 1977. *Playfulness: Its Relationship to Imagination and Creativity*. New York: Academic Press.

London, Peter. [1977] 1989. *No More Second-hand Art—Awakening the Artist Within*. Boston: Shambhala Press.

Moyer, Joan. 1989. "Whose Creation Is It, Anyway?" *Childhood Education* 66 (4): 16–22.

Piaget, J. 1962. *Play, Dreams, and Imitation in Childhood*. New York: W. W. Norton Publishing.

Read, Katherine. 1980. *The Nursery School: Human Relations and Learning*. Philadelphia: W. B. Saunders.

Rubin, K. H., K. S. Watson, and T. W. Jambor. 1978. "Free-Play Behavior in Middle and Lower Class Preschoolers: Parten and Piaget Revisited." *Child Development* 4: 414–19.

Singer, D. G. 1986. *Make-Believe and Learning, In Play: Working Partner of Growth*, ed. J. S. McKee, pp. 8–14. Wheaton, Md.: Association for Childhood Education International.

Sutton-Smith, B. 1980. "Play Isn't Just Kid's Stuff." In *Early Childhood Education 80/81*, ed. J. S. McKee. Guilford, Conn.: Dushkin Press.

Szekely, George. 1991. *Art Teaching in the Home*. Art Education—Early Childhood Anthology. Washington, D.C.: National Art Education Association.

———. 1988. *Encouraging Creativity in Art Lessons*. New York: Teachers College Press—Columbia University.

Observing and Learning from Children

Dennison, George. 1969. *The Lives of Children*. Reading, Mass.: Addison-Wesley.

Holt, John. 1983. *How Children Learn*. New York: Delta-Doubleday.

Lopate, Phillip. 1975. *Beeing with Children*. New York: Poseidon Press.

Paley, Vivian G. 1981. *Wally's Stories*. Boston: Harvard University Press.

———. 1984. *Boys and Girls*. Chicago: University of Chicago Press.

Play Programs and Ideas

Adcock, Don, and M. Segal. 1983. *Play Together—Grow Together*. New York: Mailman.

Anderson, Ken. 1990. *Games for All Occasions*. Grand Rapids, Mich.: Zendervan Press.

Ferretti, Fred. 1975. *The Great American Book of Sidewalk, Stoop, Dirt, Curb and Alley Games*. New York: Workman Publishing.

Flugelman, Andrew. 1990. *The New Games Book*. New York: Headlands Press.

Gregson, Bob. 1982. *The Incredible Indoor Plays Book*. Belmont, Calif.: Davis S. Lake Publishers.

Gordon, Alice Kaplan. 1980. *Games for Growth*. Chicago: Science Research Associates.

Hartley, J., and M. Goldenson. 1978. *The Complete Book of Children's Play*. New York: Thomas Y. Crowell.

Maguire, Jack. 1990. *Hopscotch, Hangman, Hot Potato and Ha Ha Ha*. New York: Prentice-Hall.

Marzollo, Jean. 1974. *Learning through Play*. New York: Harper and Row.

Miller, Karen. 1989. *Outside Play and Learning Book*. Baltimore: Gryphon Howe.

Press, Nancy. 1980. "Inside Art: A Program of Participation." *Art Education* 33 (1): 13–15.

Sollins, Susan. 1971. "Games Children Play in Museums." *Art Journal* 31 (3): 23–25.

Play Props and Toys

Alexander, Edwin. 1980. *Locomotives*. New York: Bramhal Howe.

Buhler, Michael. 1978. *Tin Toys 1945–1975*. New York: Quick Fox.

Billyboy. 1987. *Barbie—Her Life and Times*. Billiboy Collection. New York: Crown Publishing.

Fox, Carl. 1987. *The Doll*. New York: Abrams.

Grist, Everett. 1988. *Antique and Collectible Marbles*. Paducah, Ky.: Collector Books.

Hannas, Linda. 1981. *The Jigsaw Book*. New York: Dial Press.

Kitahara, T. 1983. *Wind-ups*. San Francisco: Chronicle Books.

———. 1985. *Robots—Tin Toy Dreams*. San Francisco: Chronicle Books.

Mandel, Margaret. 1987. *Teddy Bears and Steiff Animals*. Paducah, Ky.: Collector Books.

Musser, Cynthia Erfort. 1985. *Precious Paper Dolls*. Cumberland, Md.: Hobby House Press.

Stille, Eva. 1988. *Doll Kitchens 1800–1980*. West Chester, Pa.: Schiffler Publishing.

Striker, Susan. 1981–89. *Anti Coloring Book(s)*. 10 vol. New York: Holt, Rinehart and Winston.

Play Collections

Baker, Lilian. 1978. *Collectible Jewelry*. Paducah, Ky.: Collector Books.

Bosker, Gideon. 1986. *Great Shakes—Salt and Pepper for All Tastes*. New York: Abbeville Press.

Bruce, Scott. 1988. *Fifties and Sixties Lunch Boxes*. San Francisco: Chronicle Books.

Delano, Sharon. 1980. *Texas Boots*. New York: Penguin.

Dyer, Rod. 1987. *Vintage Ties of the Forties and Early Fifties*. New York: Abbeville Press.

Feininger, Andreas. 1983. *Shells*. New York: Dover.

Finch, Christopher. 1973. *Walt Disney*. New York: Abrams.

Fraley, Tobin. 1983. *The Carousel Animal*. Berkeley, Calif.: Zephyr Press.

Heide, Robert. 1980. *Dime Store Dream Parade: Popular Culture 1925–1955*. New York: Harper and Row.

———. 1982. *Cowboy Collectibles*. New York: Harper and Row.

Kovel, Ralph. 1981. *Book of Antique Labels*. New York: Crown.

Miles, Charles. 1980. *Indian and Eskimo Artifacts of North America*. New York: Bonanza Books.

Schiffer, Nancy. 1984. *Baskets*. Exton, Pa.: Schiffer Publishing.

Steele, H. Thomas. 1984. *The Hawaiian Shirt*. New York: Abbeville Press.

Sugar, Bert Randolph. 1978. *Hall of Fame Baseball Cards*. New York: Dover.

Wendel, Bruce, and Doranna Wendel. 1986. *Gameboards of North America*. New York: E. P. Dutton.

Performance Plays

Bohrer, Michael. 1984. *Mummenschanz*. New York: Rizzoli.

Bursill, Henry. 1977. *Hand Shadows*. New York: Dover.

Cherry, Clare. 1976. *Creative Movement for the Developing Child*. Belmont, Calif.: David S. Lake Publishers.

Finnigan, Dave. 1988. *The Complete Juggler*. New York: Vintage Press.

Kay, Drina. 1982. *All the Desk's a Stage*. Nashville, Tenn.: Incentive Publications.

Lipman, Jean. 1972. *Calder's Circus*. New York: E. P. Dutton.

Mariotti, John. 1980. *Hanimals*. San Diego, Calif.: Green Tiger Press.

Outdoor Plays

Allen, Joseph. 1981. *Sandcastles*. New York: Doubleday.

Beardsley, John. 1984. *Earth Works and Beyond*. New York: Abbeville Press.

Chalfant, Henry. 1984. *Subway Art*. New York: Holt, Rinehart and Winston.

Christo. 1982. *Complete Editions 1964–1982*. New York: New York University Press.

Clarke-Courtney, Margaret. 1987. *Ndebele*. New York: Rizzoli.

Dethier, Jean. 1983. *Down to Earth*. New York: Facts on File.

Gordon, Archie. 1979. *Towers*. London: David and Charles.

Hatton, E. M. 1979. *The Tent Book*. Boston: Houghton Mifflin.

Lippard, Lucy. 1983. *Overlay*. New York: Pantheon.

Shaffer, Carolyn, and Erica Fielder. 1982. *City Safaris*. San Francisco: Sierra Club.

Szekely, George. 1980. *Staten Island Architecture and Environment*. New York: Staten Island Museum.

Future Plays

Aero, Rita, and H. Rheingold. 1983. *New Technology*. Toronto: Bantam Books.

Asimov, Isaac. 1986. *Future Days*. New York: Henry Holt and Co.

Graves, Nancy. 1981. *Nancy Graves: A Survey 1969–1980*. Buffalo: Albright-Knox Gallery.

Hubbard, G., and T. D. Linehan. 1983. "Arcade Games, Mindstorms and Art Education." *Art Education* 36 (3): 18–20.

Hulten, K. G. 1968. *The Machine*. New York: Museum of Modern Art.

Joels, Kerry Mark. 1982. *The Space Shuttle Operators Manual*. New York: Ballantine.

Schneider, Ira, and B. Korot. 1976. *Video Art*. New York: Harcourt Brace Jovanovich.

Szekely, George. 1988. *Art Inspirations from the Computer*. Ohio Art Education Association Journal 26 (2): 8–19.

Examples for Relating Play and Art

Object plays
Rose, Barbara. 1970. *Claes Oldenburg*. New York: Museum of Modern Art.
Printing Plays
Spies, Werner. 1978. *Max Ernst Frottages*. New York: Thames and Hudson.
Cutting Plays

Elderfield, John. 1978. *The Cut-outs of Matisse*. New York: George Braziller.
Face Plays
Hirschfeld. 1979. *Hirschfeld*. New York: Dodd, Mead and Co.
Dressing-Up Plays
Rhodes, Zandra. 1985. *The Art of Zandra Rhodes*. Boston: Houghton Mifflin.
Wrapping Plays
Christo. 1982. *Complete Editions 1964–82*. New York: NYU Press.

Other Publications on Play by the Author

Szekely, G. 1991. "Discovery Experiences in Art History for Young Children." *Art Education* 44 (September): 6–12.

———. 1991. "Play, Art and Art Teaching." *Art Education—Elementary Readings*. Washington, D.C.: National Education Association.

———. 1990. "Art Teaching as a Performance." *Art Education* 43 (3): 6–18.

———. 1990. "New Approaches to Secondary School Art Education: A Program for the Artist of the Future." *Secondary Art Education: An Anthology of Issues*. Washington, D.C.: National Art Education Association.

———. 1990. "Outdoor Playing and Art." *Canadian Journal of Art Education* 21 (2): 4–11.

———. 1989. "Children's Books as an Introduction to Art." *Childhood Education* 66 (3): 132–39.

———. 1989. "Children's Drawings—A Contemporary Approach." Part 1. *School Arts* 89 (1): 14–17.

———. 1989. "Children's Drawings—A Contemporary Approach." Part 2. *School Arts*. 89 (2): 41–44.

———. 1989. *Roger Rabbit and the Movies with Young Artists*. Washington, D.C.: National Art Education Association.

———. 1988. "The Art Exhibition as a Teaching Tool." *Art Education* 41 (1): 9–18.

———. 1988. "Planning for the Sharing of Experiences and Observations." *Art Education* 41 (3): 6–13.

———. 1988. "Remote Controls, Computers, and Art Experiences." *Technological Trends* 33 (5): 20–31.

———. 1985. "Teaching Students to Understand Their Artworks." *Art Education* 38 (5): 38–44.

———. 1983. "Preliminary Play in the Art Class." *Art Education* 36 (6): 18–24.

———. 1982. "Conversations in the Art Class." *Art Education* 35 (3): 15–18.

———. 1981. "Creative Designs for Classroom Routines." *Art Education* 34 (6): 14–18.

———. 1980. "The Art Lesson as a Work Art." *Art Teacher* 10 (3): 12–15.

———. 1979. "Childhood Play and the School Art Program." *Art Teacher* 9 (2): 14–17.

———. 1977. "Toy Design as an Introduction to Sculpture." *Arts and Activities* 82 (3): 18–22.

Index

Index